The
Little
Book
of
Pintfulness

The Little Book of Pintfulness

HOWARD LINSKEY

The History Press

This book is dedicated to master practitioners of Pintfulness: Adam Pope, Andy Davis, Chris Tole and Gareth Chennells. Cheers lads!

First published 2020

The History Press
97 St George's Place, Cheltenham,
Gloucestershire, GL50 3QB
www.thehistorypress.co.uk

British Library Cataloguing in Publication Data.
A catalogue record for this book is available from the British Library.

ISBN 978 0 7509 9466 8
Typesetting and origination by The History Press
Printed and bound in Great Britain by TJ International Ltd.

Cover Illustration © Jemma Cox
Internal images © Freepik.com

It matters not if the glass is half full or half empty,
only whether there is enough time left to refill it.

Dr Pivo Cerveza de Bibere,
Emeritus Professor of Pintfulness,
Huddersfield Polytechnic

Pintfulness *(noun)*

The art of being 'in the pint'

THE NEED FOR PINTFULNESS:
SNOWFLAKE JIBES AND MEANINGLESS MINDFULNESS

We all need Pintfulness, but no one more so than the young, who seem to have forgotten all about it. I feel sorry for the youth of today, I genuinely do. Young people don't drink anything like as much as their parents and grandparents. They grew up witnessing the effects it had on them and inwardly cringed as Mummy fell over at the BBQ under the influence of Prosecco and Dad decided to show off his dance moves after eight pints of Doom Bar.

Instead of blowing their pocket money on bottles of cider to drink behind garages or blagging their way into pubs clutching fake IDs, millennials and post-millennials were already on their way to premature adulthood by their mid teens. These days, young people are weighed down with worry about uncertain futures, exam results, college applications, housing prices, the state of the world and global warming. Then there's the hopelessness of ever landing a job that comes with even the most basic benefits that their parents took for granted. A pension? We closed those for new entrants years ago. Paid holiday? You're freelance, there's no such thing. A pay rise, when we can replace you with an unpaid intern? Get a second or third job. Uber always need someone and Deliveroo are hiring. Add in the low likelihood of ever having a sexual relationship that doesn't involve webcamming naked strangers in their bedrooms, and you can see why young people might be depressed.

They are constantly told to check their privilege, avoid cultural appropriation, and become fully woke before they open their mouths. A simple conversation is a linguistic minefield that can lead to social exclusion and pariah status.

Even ordering lunch is no longer a simple matter. It used to be a ham or cheese sandwich, maybe egg mayonnaise if you really wanted to be different, but now it has to be gluten-free, vegetarian, vegan, or possibly even 'pegan' (yes, it's a thing – I despair – look it up). Somewhere between half a million and a million people in this country are now vegan and face each day with the deliberate intention of avoiding the joys of a bacon sandwich. My heart aches for them.

Social media makes millennials feel wretched, in comparison to their better-looking, more popular, more successful mates, and they can't afford a tiny corner of a shared bedsit to live in. Meanwhile, the *Daily Mail* encourages thousands of older people to call them 'snowflakes' who can't handle the real world.

It's not sufficient to go to the gym once a week anymore. Instead, you have to have a personal trainer (someone you actually pay to make you feel bad) or sign up for a 'boot camp', as if you were preparing to join the Paras and fight in Afghanistan, not simply navigate your way around Sainsbury's with a squeaky trolley. You can't just go for a walk either. Instead, you are bullied into triathlons, iron man challenges or Tough Mudder events, because exercise is too easy unless you are knee deep in mud. Then you must make time for yourself, to cultivate a mindfulness at odds with your frazzled state. Oh, and don't forget to Instagram all of the above or none of it counts.

Not for them the simple pleasure of unwinding with a pint of bitter and a packet of crisps. If you believe what's written about them, the only toast millennials are likely to propose is the sourdough kind – but only if it has crushed avocado on it. Their self-control and maturity is incredible. They are an eminently sensible breed of serious, health-conscious, gym-obsessed teetotallers, who also happen to be the most stressed and anxiety-ridden generation to have walked the planet.

This is no coincidence.

All is not lost for this most unfortunate of generations however, nor anyone else from a later one who – through overwork, stress or an absence of calm in their lives – has lost their peace of mind. Read on and discover how to get it back.

REGAINING THE LOST
ART OF PINTFULNESS

Every day another horde of self-proclaimed experts will tell you how to reboot your life, detox your system, cleanse your soul or align your chakras (whatever they are), and though you may be tempted to listen to the latest jogger, blogger or vlogger spouting some new age nonsense (as long as you pay for it, natch), deep down, you know it's mostly bollocks, right? And, even if it *isn't*, you haven't got the time to shop for the Lycra-filled wardrobe needed to take part in it all.

Most of these therapies will be forgotten as quickly as the name of the last leader of the Lib Dems. The true road to enlightenment can only be found on the most ancient of pathways, and we have been perfecting this one for around 7,000 years. We know where we are with Pintfulness, though many have sadly forgotten. Within the pages of this book lies the all-important wisdom required to regain this lost art.

In a post-Brexit apocalyptic world, likely to resemble the opening scenes from *Mad Max Fury Road*, the futility of an existence without Pintfulness might finally and belatedly be realised. Take a leaf out of earlier generations and adopt the mantra that was often spoken after a long, hard day: 'Fuck it, I'm off to the pub.'

THE HARD FACTS OF BEER

Think about this for a moment, preferably while holding a pint and gazing out of the window of a pub:

- Beer is the third most popular drink on the planet.
- The only more widely consumed liquids are water and tea.

There are millions of teetotal people in the world, for moral, health or religious reasons. Muslims, for example, typically don't consume alcohol because it is haram (forbidden) in Islamic law and they make up approximately 24 per cent of the planet's population. So, even though it is only consumed by three quarters of the population, beer is still right behind water (consumed by everyone, including kids) and tea (which is not forbidden anywhere).

It is quite staggering that beer is still more popular than coffee, a beverage that is far more socially acceptable to consume at breakfast or in the office. Caffeine might be a drug, but it is regarded as a minor one. Most people feel they can kickstart their morning with it without facing eternal damnation.

Water has another big advantage over beer in that it costs nothing. In our country we pay water rates but tend not to think of that when consuming tap water for drinking. Generally, people in the UK clutch single-use, plastic water bottles to their person almost as tightly as their mobile phones. The average cost of tap water in this country is 0.1p per litre, whereas a bottle of water will set you back anything between 65p and well over a quid, depending on how evil the individual retailer is.

Beer, on the other hand, costs considerably more and that's partially the fault of the taxman. The average cost of a pint of bitter in the UK in 2019 was £3.69 – more than the cost of five single-use bottles of water purchased individually.

The cheapest place to drink in UK pubs was in Shropshire or Herefordshire, at around £3.37 a pint. The most expensive was, of course, London, where the price was an eyewatering £4.44 per pint – up by 24p on the previous year.

The taxman gets 54p from every pint of normal strength beer you purchase; nearly 15 per cent of the money you hand to the landlord. We pay fourteen times more tax on our beer than German drinkers.

Despite its cost contributing to young people eschewing beer in the UK, its popularity worldwide is still consistently and reassuringly high.

THE MOTHER OF ALL INVENTIONS

He was a wise man who invented beer.

Plato

Who invented beer? No, seriously, I'd love to know. This guy ought to be a household name, up there with Shakespeare and Churchill (more of whom later), but instead their identity has been lost in the mists of time.

We know that beer was invented at least 5,000 years ago but not who *by*, and it is likely that a number of cultures began brewing things to create an intoxicating effect at roughly the same time.

Perhaps the bigger question should be *how* was beer invented? It seems like such a long shot to occur by accident that it begs the question: how did someone come up with this from scratch deliberately?

Cooking is easier to understand. Some careless caveman dozed off by the fire and that morning's kill fell into it while he was asleep. Soon his raw meat was cooked and, after the bollocking he got from his other half for being the first man in history to burn his dinner, everyone figured it would be a shame to waste it and tucked in anyway. Imagine the eye-popping moment when their raw wild boar accidentally became roast pork and they got to taste it for the first time. I'm guessing a while later they invented apple sauce and never looked back.

Brewing, however, is more complex – though it is possible primitive man accidentally allowed some fruit or barley to brew or ferment before getting pleasantly shit-faced on the results. This happy accident, many moons ago, eventually led to what we now call the brewing industry. In fact, man's innate ability to sit back, put his feet up and sip a pint dates back to at least 5,000 BCE (Before Common Era, or Before Christ, if you prefer that). We know this because the earliest recipe known to man goes back that far and it wasn't for a ham and cheese toastie. It was for beer.

Yes, beer.

This discovery is up there with the idea that the two oldest professions are spying and prostitution, in that it is slightly shocking but makes perfect sense. Basically, we know that ancient man was a lot like us. There he was, going about the business of surviving while trying to earn a living and attempting to ease the stress of low wages and high taxes, with a large cup of some intoxicating brew. He knew what I know: life is just better with beer.

So, where and when was the art of Pintfulness first practised? Ironically, the earliest recorded reference to the brewing of beer comes from Iran, a nation of humourless teetotallers if ever there was one.

WATER MY BEER AND DIE!

Hammurabi was a ruler in ancient Babylon (a civilisation that emerged in Mesopotamia from the ashes of the Sumerians) and he took beer very seriously indeed. He is best known for a series of laws known, unsurprisingly, as the 'Code of Hammurabi'. Some of the oldest, lengthiest writings in history, they established rules concerning a number of things that Hammurabi felt strongly about. Ruling way back between 1792 and 1750 BCE, you might not have expected him to be quite so precise about everything, but his code of law was comprehensive. There were 282 laws that each came with specific punishments for breaking them. They included the amount that should be paid to certain workers, liability for a faulty building, divorce and inheritance rules, and the manner in which a woman could take her dowry and leave her husband if she was wronged.

The ahead-of-his-time Hammurabi gets a mention here because he included rules on the brewing of beer. He wanted to ensure no one had the temerity to water down his ale. Brewers back in those days often used inferior ingredients and added water to their mixture. Hammurabi must have tasted the results and became rightly incensed. Under his law, if you watered down beer then the penalty was death! I'm usually pretty liberal-minded but, in this instance, I'm in full agreement with the man. Is there a bigger crime? I doubt it!

With a poetic twist, the offender wasn't hanged or beheaded but, with an irony the condemned must surely have appreciated, they were sentenced to be drowned in their own watery beer.

THE COMPETITION, DEBUNKED AND DISMISSED

YOGA

Yoga is often called an ancient practice, but it dates back to a mere five centuries BCE. That means it has been around for 2,500 years but it's only half as old as the first recipe for beer. How can you trust something so new?

Yoga originated in ancient India, but it has splintered into so many different types that you have to ask yourself why. There is classical yoga, Buddhist yoga, Jain yoga, Vedanta yoga, tantric yoga, hatha yoga, laya yoga and Kundalini yoga. Basically, no one can agree on the right way to do it. Nearly everyone agrees on the right way to drink beer and that it's basically a good thing, so beer wins.

There is also the problem of yoga farts. Google it: there are many references to the side effect of relaxing your body to such a degree – farting during yoga is pretty common. Now I realise that beery farts can also be a bit of an issue, but it is not common for someone to shatter the tranquillity of a quiet pub with a loud, rasping fart.

PILATES

Basically just yoga with a more modern name. Much beloved of trendy yummy mummies with more money than sense, Pilates is every-bloody-where.

It was invented by a German prisoner called Joseph Pilates in the First World War while he was stuck in an internment camp on the Isle of Man. As it took almost a hundred years to catch on, it can't have been *that* amazing. Forget banning plastic lids and cups to save the environment, just forbid the production of all those colourful leaflets that are pushed through letter boxes on a weekly basis by desperate Pilates teachers.

As I write this, the average cost of a Pilates class is between four to six times the price of a pint of beer. You do the maths. In fact, don't bother because I just did it for you. Beer wins again.

MINDFULNESS

Mindfulness might be the better-known counterpart to Pintfulness, but it is a hell of a lot newer, having only reached any level of public attention in the early '90s. My strong suspicion is that, if it wasn't needed until then, it's probably not needed now.

The mindfulness message is staggeringly simple, to the point where I am at a loss as to why you would need to buy a book about it. Yet there are dozens of tomes, read by thousands of people with too much time on their hands. Basically, the mindfulness message can be distilled down to being 'in the moment'. That's it.

No, I am not pulling your leg. An entire industry, employing huge numbers of people and generating millions of pounds, has been set up on the premise of 'living in the now'. That could mean turning your attention to the single drop of rainwater slowly sliding down your window, focusing on its gradual descent to facilitate a sense of calm and well-being. What a load of bollocks.

Prior to the 1990s, this would accurately be called daydreaming. You could get fired for that as an adult, or if you were younger, have a chalk duster thrown directly and forcefully at your head by your teacher for not paying attention to their mind-numbing Geography lessons.

Other advice is to use meditation until a state of mindfulness is ultimately achieved. The very same level of calmness can be reached if a pint is purchased and taken to a quiet corner of a dimly lit (but characterful) pub, where the mind is allowed to declutter itself while gentle sips of the rejuvenating ale are taken.

Pintfulness is an older and better form of mindfulness – and it includes beer.

BEING 'IN THE PINT'

The one thing that the supremely overrated mindfulness has in common with Pintfulness is the ability to be truly in the moment. The next time you walk into your local, don't be impatient as you stand at the bar, waiting for that old bloke to count all his coins on it before he hands them over as payment to harassed bar staff. Avoid the temptation to tut or grind your teeth while the person next to you tries and fails to work out what they want. Instead, adopt a zen-like attitude towards the soothing inevitabilities: you will eventually be served, and a good pint is always worth the wait.

Remind yourself that there is no better place to be than here right now, patiently waiting. You could be at work, queuing at the bank (older people still do this) or stuck in traffic on the M25. This is your natural habitat, take a moment to enjoy it. Be 'in the pint'.

DITHER YE NOT: DECISION TIME

Because you are a Professor of Pintfulness, or will be once you have read the wise words in this book, you will have already worked out what you want before speaking to the bar staff. This applies even when the list of bitters on offer is long and features names like Wellington Bomber, Witches' Piss and Elf's Chunder – half of which you've never heard of. Why people who create beer, and by definition must be Professors of Pintfulness, inflict these gimmicky epithets on drinkers is beyond me.

A good beer should have a strong but simple name, without being overburdened with historical baggage or cheapened by Lord of the Rings style elvish fuckery. It's at best a distraction and at worst puts me off their brew entirely. Drinking a pint is a serious, almost religious, experience but a true state of grace cannot be achieved while drinking Dragon's Phlegm.

By the time it's your turn, you will have scanned the pumps and checked out the original gravity on each beer, to avoid accidentally ordering something with 9 per cent alcohol. You will have found a brewery you are vaguely aware of and worked out which ale looks best to avoid because it is likely to make you wince when you sip it. You will have done all of this because no one likes a ditherer, especially in a pub. It's acceptable to ask a question or two about a beer's qualities, but only if the room is quiet. When there is a queue at the bar, forget it.

If you are still in doubt, simply ask the bar staff to give you a pint of whatever they sell the most of. You will be safe in the knowledge that many previous customers have already road tested it for you and they can't all be wrong.

THE MOMENT OF POUR

Admire the dedication and professionalism of the bartender as they take up a stance not that dissimilar to one of Henry V's stout English archers at the Battle of Agincourt: feet apart, one slightly behind the other for balance; a firm grip on the pump; then a slight brace as they draw back their 'pulling-arm' (I'll resist the temptation to make cheap masturbation jokes here).

Notice how, like many experienced bartenders, they will have one bicep slightly bigger than the other. Note too the angle of the glass, which is largely dependent on how gassy the beer is, then observe the dark, rejuvenating liquid as they draw back the pump and it begins to flow. For a state of true Pintfulness, you should now be lost in 'the moment of Pour', as the beer swirls under pressure, fighting for its rightful space in the glass, even as it is joined by more of the same.

Watch the bartender right the glass towards the end to avoid spillage, then keep your eyes on the pint as they complete the pour and rest it on the bar in front of you.

SETTLING

This is one of the key moments of Pintfulness, yet it is often overlooked in man's haste to complete transactions and move onward, ever onward, in the pointless haste of life. The forgivable interruption from the busy bar staff, demanding the cost of the beer, should not distract you from enjoying the pint as it slowly settles.

Hand them the money – or press your little plastic card across the machine, if you like using such newfangled technology. Me? I prefer a wallet full of notes, so I'm not robbed of the simple pleasure of walking home with half a tonne of shrapnel in my pocket, because I change one of those notes every time I buy a round. Unexpectedly finding twenty quid's worth of pound coins in my pocket in the morning always makes me feel like I won the jackpot in an ancient pub's fruit machine.

You have your change/have swiped your card? Good. Now, let the moisture slide from the outside of the glass onto the bar towel before picking it up. Admire its clarity but don't hold it high in front of you to gaze adoringly at it as if it's a precious jewel chipped from the Koh-i-noor diamond, lest you look like a twat.

Don't take your eye from the pint as it settles. Imagine the swirling mass in your glass represents the inner turmoil in your life that will soon be calmed, for a moment or two at least. Enjoy the anticipation as the beer begins to settle and draw a direct parallel in your mind between it and your heart rate, blood pressure and stress levels.

Take the pint to a quiet corner. It is now settled and so are you.

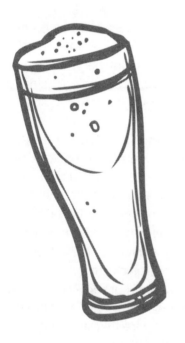

THE BEER NECESSITIES:
DO BEARS DRINK IN THE WOODS?

You don't have to be human to be a Professor of Pintfulness. Even bears appreciate the value of a good beer.

According to the Washington Department of Fish and Wildlife, a black bear broke into empty tents at the Swift Creek Campground. That is not an uncommon occurrence in the backwoods of the USA, but usually they forage for food. This one had a better idea. He found someone's stash of beer and started drinking; he didn't finish until he had demolished thirty-six cans. The bear got drunk (unsurprisingly after three dozen tinnies) and then passed out.

Unfortunately, the culprit did not get away with the crime, because the bear wasn't very good at covering his tracks. A few clues were left behind, including a handy trail of empty beer cans. Each one had claw and bite marks in it, so there was no need to dust for fingerprints. You didn't have to be a detective to solve this one. At the end of the beery trail they found the heavily inebriated bear and, if the evidence wasn't already damning enough, he was staggering. Unable to run away, he sensibly decided to climb up a tree and sleep it off before making an escape.

The bear's story has a bittersweet ending though. He came back the next day, just as they suspected he might, but this time a trap had been set. If you are imagining that it was large and made of sharp metal, the truth was (thankfully) far less dramatic. This one consisted of bait including doughnuts, honey and two cans of his favourite beer. It did the trick and the bear was captured safely before being relocated a safe distance away from campers.

The best part of the story wasn't *what* the bear did but *how* he went about it. He discovered two brands of beer in the tents. The bear tasted one and didn't like it very much. Rather like an inverted tale of Goldilocks, he then tried the other and found that it was 'just right', so he never went back to the first brand. Yes, this bear was a discerning drinker. For the record, he didn't like Busch Beer but was a fan of Rainier. I don't know why the Rainier marketing people haven't come up with a campaign focused entirely on the fact that their beer is the choice of the discerning bear, but I think they are missing a trick.

LIQUID BREAD
(BEER IS GOOD FOR YOU)

Beer will save your life – well, it did in the Middle Ages and it wasn't just because it was nutritious. If you had a sip of water back then you were taking your life in your own hands. People bathed, pissed and washed clothes in the river, with little awareness of germs and their consequences. Water was far more dangerous back then. It was impure and often contained the source of potentially fatal illnesses like cholera, typhoid or dysentery. However, the water used in brewing is boiled and the rest of the beer-making process kills germs and rids the beer of bacteria.

Beer is also more nutritious than water due to its additional ingredients. It could be kept much longer than fresh produce, which went off quickly in a world before refrigeration or canned foods.

With a lower strength than present-day beers, ale could be consumed in large quantities and at all times of the day. The fact that it contained virtually the same ingredients as bread made it an important part of most people's daily nutrition. No wonder beer used to be referred to as 'liquid bread'.

SMALL BEER:
BEER FOR BREAKFAST

He's small beer. It's small beer. We've all heard that expression and think we know what it means. He or it is unimportant. We are describing something inconsequential in the world – but that's not the original meaning of the phrase. Long before 'small beer' was used as a minor insult, it was actually a valued part of a worker's diet and even a child's daily nutrition.

We've already discussed how insanitary water could (and often did) kill you, so the process of brewing beer was actually a lifesaver. This meant that virtually everyone drank beer, including kids and those involved in heavy manual labour.

However, even back then it was not considered wise to get kids drunk, and most people doubted the sanity of sending stonemasons to the giddy heights at the top of a cathedral if they were pissed. It wasn't uncommon for workers to drink as many as ten pints of the stuff during a working day in order to quench their thirst, so it's a wonder anyone survived at all or that any actual work got done.

The answer to the problem was 'small beer', which was a description of beer brewed with much less alcohol. This ale would typically have an original gravity of only 1 per cent – just as well if the kids were quaffing it for breakfast; a practice normally reserved for more grown-up participants of stag dos before they board short-haul flights to inexpensive cities in Eastern Europe.

THE WORLD'S BIGGEST BEER DRINKERS

ANDRE THE GIANT

Who was the biggest drinker of beer ever? That's one of those questions that is impossible to answer, right? I mean, beer drinking has been going on for millennia, all over the world, and a great deal of it happens without witnesses, apart from the drinker's closest mates, many of whom are just as drunk as the person doing most of the drinking. Truly legendary tales of beer consumption are rarely witnessed by anyone remotely credible, let alone a representative of the *Guinness Book of Records*, and the reports are prone to exaggeration. Eight pints becomes ten, a dozen becomes fifteen and so on.

However, there is one man whose drinking exploits were so frequent and so legendary that they were witnessed by many. He is a strong and credible candidate for the world's biggest ever drinker of beer. Andre the Giant (real name André René Roussimoff) was famous as a wrestler in America, thanks to massive sell-out bouts against the likes of Hulk Hogan in the WWF in the eighties. In Europe, the French-born fighter was probably best known for his scene-stealing appearance as Fezzik, the enormous henchman in Rob Reiner's classic film *The Princess Bride*. Lately, his fame as a drinker on a simply epic scale has threatened to eclipse both his acting and wrestling careers.

As his name might suggest, Andre the Giant was an enormous fellow. He suffered from gigantism, where problems with growth hormones cause excessive growth; he was more than 6ft 3in tall by the time he was 12, and already weighed in at 208lb. As an adult his size was disputed, but it was generally accepted that he was well over 7ft tall, possibly even 7ft 4in.

Andre had a thirst to match his size, which is why he has to be included in any serious study of Pintfulness, even if his contribution is at the extreme end of the scale, and readers should definitely not try to emulate him at home.

I don't have the time or the space to detail all of his gargantuan drinking sessions here, so I am going to focus on just one: the night Andre consumed more than seventy pints in one session. Seventy!

It took him approximately six hours to polish off 119 bottles of American beer. I know this tends to taste more watery than UK beer, but I couldn't drink 119 of them. He finally passed out in the lobby of his hotel, but he was so big no one could move him. They left him there to sleep it off until morning.

Despite being a legendary pisshead and a fearsome fighter, Andre was apparently a gentle soul in real life. Because of his size, the poor man had a variety of health problems throughout his life and his heart eventually gave out when he was just 47 years old. I think it's fair to say he got the most from a short life and lived it to the max.

COUNTRIES

Individually, Andre the Giant may have been the world's biggest beer drinker, but if we look at drinking as a team sport then we can identify entire nations filled with complete ale heads.

You'd kind of expect the Brits to be pretty high up in that list, wouldn't you? What with the dull and rainy climate and our sad, unfulfilled lives, full of long and stressful Americanised working conditions and you would be ... wrong!

Actually, the biggest beer drinkers in the world, per capita, are to be found in the Czech Republic. The average Czech consumes around 208 pints a year to top a league table they have been champions of for twenty-five years, and they show no sign of ever relinquishing their crown. To be honest, if I lived in a country that had invented Staropramen, Budweiser Budvar (not to be confused with the watery American equivalent) and Pilsner Urquell, I would drink more too.

But who gets the runners-up spot? Namibia, obviously.

Yeah, really, Namibia. Who'd have thunk it? The only explanation for this peculiar cultural foible is its ancient colonial links with Germany – which brings us neatly to the impressive level of Germanic beer consumption.

In third and fourth place are the Austrians and Germans. No surprise there. They take their beer drinking very seriously and there is even a famous German beer purity law to ensure no one messes with an important part of the Germanic diet. The *Reinheitsgebot* has been around since the year 1516 and specifies the ingredients that may be used in the brewing of beer. The only ones allowed are water, barley and hops. Even yeast doesn't get a mention, because back then its role in fermentation was unknown. The law was later amended to permit its inclusion.

The Poles clinch fifth spot in the league of beery boozers, which is perhaps unsurprising for a nation historically sandwiched between (and fought over by) Germany and Russia, and which only achieved liberation in the late eighties. They had a lot to drink about.

Ireland is only sixth in this league! Did they forget to include Guinness in their calculations? That must surely be the only explanation. If you are drinking more than the Irish it's probably time to go home.

Gloomy Eastern European nations Romania, Lithuania and Estonia make up the top ten, along with, rather more surprisingly, The Seychelles, proving that people will reach for the consolation of ale even in a tourist paradise.

So, where does Britain lie in this league of shame/pride*? You, like me, will most likely be flabbergasted to learn that, in the list of the world's biggest beer drinkers, Britain does not even make it into the top twenty. I thought we'd be top three at least!

It just goes to show how far we have slipped in the eyes of others and ourselves. We can't even break into the league table of biggest pissheads. Oh, how the mighty have fallen.

* depending on your outlook.

THE GERMAN BEER LAWS:
THE *REINHEITSGEBOT* IN FULL

The text (translated) of the 1516 Bavarian law is as follows:

We hereby proclaim and decree, by Authority of our Province, that henceforth in the Duchy of Bavaria, in the country as well as in the cities and marketplaces, the following rules apply to the sale of beer:

From Michaelmas to Georgi, the price for one Mass [Bavarian Litre] or one Kopf [bowl-shaped container for fluids, not quite one Mass], is not to exceed one Pfennig Munich value, and From Georgi to Michaelmas, the Mass shall not be sold for more than two Pfennig of the same value, the Kopf not more than three Heller [Heller was usually one-half Pfennig].

If this not be adhered to, the punishment stated below shall be administered.

Should any person brew, or otherwise have, other beer than March beer, it is not to be sold any higher than one Pfennig per Mass.

Furthermore, we wish to emphasize that in future in all cities, market-towns and in the country, the only ingredients used for the brewing of beer must be Barley, Hops and Water. Whosoever knowingly disregards or transgresses upon this ordinance, shall be punished by the Court authorities' confiscating such barrels of beer, without fail.

Should, however, an innkeeper in the country, city or market-towns buy two or three pails of beer (containing

60 Mass) and sell it again to the common peasantry, he alone shall be permitted to charge one Heller more for the Mass or the Kopf, than mentioned above. Furthermore, should there arise a scarcity and subsequent price increase of the barley (also considering that the times of harvest differ, due to location), WE, the Bavarian Duchy, shall have the right to order curtailments for the good of all concerned.

And there you have it: German organisation at its finest, with control over not just the ingredients of beer but the amount and time of its supply, along with the price that should be charged. Thankfully for German brewers, they have been allowed to move with the times and can charge more than a couple of pfennigs for it these days.

BEER FOR LIFE:
THE REAL NOBEL PRIZE

Niels Bohr was a cool guy. The Danish physicist's understanding of quantum theory led to him winning the Nobel Prize way back in 1922. That makes him a very clever man but not necessarily a dude. His claim to cool fame came slightly later.

The Carlsberg brewery were so impressed that one of their countrymen had won such an internationally prestigious award that they decided to give him an even bigger prize. First, they presented Niels with a house, close to the brewery – but even that generous gift is not the cool bit. They then arranged to have his new home connected to the brewery via a pipeline and ensured he had an uninterrupted supply of free draft beer for life.

Carlsberg has a well-known advertising campaign these days, all about what they don't do. Perhaps they should tell everybody what they *did* do for Niels. It would give fellow Danes a pretty big incentive to emulate his Nobel-winning feat.

DROWNING IN BEER:
THE LONDON BEER FLOOD OF 1814

We've all heard of the Great Fire of London: a monumental blaze in 1666 that destroyed 13,000 houses, 87 churches (including St Paul's Cathedral) and completely reshaped London.

Slightly less well known than the Great Fire is the much less talked about London Beer Flood of 1814, but in one crucial way it was even more serious – and I am not referring to the heartbreaking loss of 323,000 gallons of beer.

If you are struggling to imagine any circumstances that could have caused an actual flood of beer to swamp the streets of London, then read on and be suitably enlightened.

You're possibly thinking that this can't have been a very big deal for anyone but the brewery, certainly compared to the aforementioned Great Fire. It's true to say that only three buildings were affected by the beer torrent after all. However, there is one incredible fact that puts this tragedy into true perspective. More people were killed in the little-known Beer Flood than in the notorious Great Fire.

On 17 October 1814, in the Parish of St Giles, Meux & Co. was expecting an uneventful day at their brewery in Tottenham Court Road – then a massive vat filled with 135,000 gallons of beer suddenly ruptured and all hell broke loose. The explosion of beer caused other vats to topple over and they too released their contents. Soon there was a tidal wave of beer so large and powerful that it destroyed two houses and smashed down a wall of the nearby Tavistock Arms, killing Eleanor Cooper, a young employee. Two more people were killed as the beer flowed unstoppably into the streets.

Perhaps the fatalities would have ended there, after the immediate torrent, if it were not for the way people lived back then. Nearby buildings had basements that were used by families as living quarters. A further five people drowned as a result of the beer rapidly flooding into these basements.

Not a penny in compensation was paid to the families of any of the victims, because the tragedy was considered an act of God. By the end of the flood, a total of eight people had been killed, including three children under the age of 5. The Great Fire of London, for all its devastation to property and historical significance, resulted in a mere six fatalities.

BEER BORES

These guys are to be avoided at all cost.

It is okay to care about the quality of your pint, but when you turn your craft-beer drinking into an obsessive analysis of hops and original gravity, as well as an unceasing quest not only to sample the most obscure and undrinkable brews but to *tell* people about it, then you have a problem. Said problem won't be that you have too many friends, or even any by this point, except fellow saddos.

Beer bores will happily pay seven quid for a pint of dark, flat ale that tastes like it was brewed through a sweaty sock filled with peat chiselled from a North Yorkshire moor. They would never deign to consider a pint of unspectacular but perfectly acceptable draft brand beer. Worshipping ales that come at a prohibitive cost with an acrid taste is the Pintfulness equivalent of applauding an emperor as he rides by without a stitch of clothing on his person.

THE STRANGER'S BAR:
THE POLITICS OF BEER

Such is the talismanic effect of a pint that these days virtually every politician makes a point of being photographed holding one, in order to con us all into believing that they are 'one of us'. If this had a name it should be probably called the 'Farage Effect'.

It's almost unheard of for Nigel Farage not to be seen clutching a pint, and I have it on a very good authority that he far prefers beer to a milkshake. Farage knows that if he is pictured standing in a pub sipping a beer, then a fair percentage of our country's population will pronounce him 'alright', as if the ability to drink beer outweighs rampant xenophobia and all round political twattishness. The constant pint-swigging is possibly the only explanation as to why a former stockbroker, worth millions, is able to carry off the act of pretending to be a man of the people and a thorn in the side of the 'political elites'.

Farage is of course immensely popular with anyone slightly to the right of Mussolini, but not all of the general public have been fooled by the beer-drinking image. He has contested seven parliamentary elections in his quest to become an MP and lost the lot.

SOME CORNER OF A FOREIGN FIELD: THE CHINA CRISIS

The power of Pintfulness in British politics is so strong it is even used in international diplomacy. When then Prime Minister David Cameron received a visit to the UK from Chinese President Xi Jinping in 2015, the formality of welcoming the autocratic leader of a potentially hostile superpower was lessened by a trip to Cameron's favourite boozer, The Plough.

This sixteenth-century pub in Cadston, Buckinghamshire, served up pints of IPA and fish and chips to a possibly bemused Chinese leader and it all went down a storm back home. So much so that the Chinese flexed their not-insubstantial financial muscle and promptly bought the place. The Chinese government-backed investment group SinoFortone now own Cameron's old local, which is a short distance from his former prime ministerial home of Chequers. Talk about parking their tanks on his lawn; I bet he didn't see that coming! Now it gets busloads of curious Chinese tourists and is the model for a chain of English-style pubs in their homeland.

The Far East's fascination with all things Pintfulness doesn't stop there. Li Ka-Shing, Hong Kong's richest man and founder of the company CKA, is the new owner of massive UK brewery chain Greene King, the nation's biggest pub landlord. CKA paid £2.7 billion for its 2,700 UK pubs, while also picking up its debts of a mere £1.9 billion, as part of the deal.

Japan has also expressed an interest in British brewing assets. Asahi bought the Chiswick brewery Fullers for £250 million.

Fullers was founded way back in 1845 and was family run until 2019, when Asahi stepped in and snapped it up.

In the meantime, sales of IPA are booming in China, thanks to that meeting between their president and David Cameron, and the UK-style pubs are prospering. We might have become a tiny and inconsequential country compared to China, but thanks to Pintfulness, it is true to say, as Rupert Brooke put it: 'That there's some corner of a foreign field that is for ever England.'

A YARD OF ALE

To those of you unfamiliar with a yard of ale, it is a very tall, approximately yard-long thin glass, with a bulb at the bottom that can contain around two and half pints or one and a half litres of beer. This might seem excessive, possibly even extremely foolish, when you then take into account that this enormous measure of ale is meant to be drunk in a single, uninterrupted sip.

Dating back to the seventeenth century, the yard of ale is said to have been invented for the purpose of assisting coach drivers to get refreshment without having to leave their perch on the top of the coach. Like an F1 driver at a pitstop, for him speed is of the essence. The idea is that while the needs of the horses are attended to, the coach driver would be handed this huge measure, of around a quart of ale, in a glass long enough for him to hold and down it while still in place.

If this tale sounds improbable to you, don't worry, it is almost certainly a myth. The yard of ale was most likely constructed initially as a showy way to make a special toast to the king and there is historical record of this. Later, it naturally evolved into a test of drinking prowess, a dare or (most often) a punishment or forfeit at predominantly young, male gatherings, such as college sporting teams.

The feat of downing all of the beer is rendered even harder by the bulb at the bottom of the glass, which practically guarantees you a rush of beer when you need it least, and you are likely to end up wearing some of it.

The current world record for consuming a yard of ale, held by Peter Dowdeswell, is a stomach-stretching five seconds.

GIVE HIM AN INCH: BOB HAWKE

I could easily fit the next fella into the politics category because, on his own admission, beer played a massive part in his rise to the very top of the political tree, but I'm going to leave him here, because he has secured his place in history.

Bob Hawke was Australian Prime Minister between 1983 and 1991, and was one of the country's most famous politicians. A legendary drinker and womaniser, he was also the holder of the world record for downing a yard of ale.

When Hawke was a Rhodes Scholar at the University of Oxford, he was given a forfeit by fellow students for some misdemeanour and ordered to drink from a traditional Sconce pot. Being 'sconced' was a common punishment for crimes such as talking about religion, work or women, or making a breach of etiquette of some kind during dinner.

Hawke's sconcing achieved legendary status, when he successfully downed the equivalent of two and a half pints (a yard of ale) in just eleven seconds, earning him the then world record for the feat. Some politicians look back on the wildness of their youth and cringe, but Hawke was clearly and understandably proud of his achievement, citing that it probably benefited his political career in Australia more than anything else he did, because it endeared him to an Aussie public who had a natural respect for beer-drinking prowess.

Bob Hawke achieved a lot as a politician, but they say all political careers end in failure; sure enough, he was eventually ousted by fellow Labour politician, Paul Keating. Any bitterness he may have felt about this betrayal from his long-term political partner must surely have been softened when he retired from politics completely and went into business, safe in the knowledge that his world record for skulling a sconce of ale could never be erased by a leadership defeat.

PINTFULNESS TO EXCESS

WE SHALL DRINK IN THE PUBS AND IN THE BARS: WINSTON CHURCHILL

Every family has one, right? That old auntie or elderly great-uncle; the one who imbibes way more than your average or recommended weekly alcohol consumption in a single evening, pausing only to smoke their way through three packets of fags a day. They then contrive to confound medical opinion by living to 104. Meanwhile, those who adopt a more sensible approach to drinking drop like flies. There's really no justice.

The political equivalent of that great-uncle was Winston Churchill, who took the concept of Pintfulness to such an extreme degree that he is now generally regarded as a functioning alcoholic. So much so that the Churchill Project website has defended him, by saying that he really wasn't that big a drinker, honest – then accidentally damning him with their own evidence. According to them, Churchill drank to excess but wasn't actually an alcy. They don't mention how much beer he drank but he did consume an average of 'a pint' of wine or champagne a day for lunch and another pint for dinner, which translates as four glasses of wine per meal or eight every day. He also consumed between nine and twelve whiskeys a day, plus a couple of brandies.

Churchill was a flawed but great leader who led our country through its darkest hour and should be rightly eulogised for that – but let's be honest here; he was an absolute pisshead.

No wonder he thought he could outfight the Nazi war machine. If I drank that much every day, I'd probably think I could fight Tyson Fury.

Imagine having *four* glasses of champagne for lunch then returning to the office. You wouldn't be trusted to make the tea without scalding yourself. Then he did it all *again* in the evening. Incredible and certainly not to be recommended. The fact that he went on for another twenty years and died in 1965, at the grand old age of 90, makes him something of a medical miracle. Most people's major organs would shut down when exposed to so much booze, but I can only assume that Winnie's were preserved somehow in a process reminiscent of the pickling of fruit to make chutney.

I always thought that his staggering confidence, when all about him were anticipating ignominious defeat and pondering the terms of a negotiated capitulation to the Germans, was down to some inner strength others lacked. But maybe he was just hammered. Did he prowl the bunker of the Cabinet War Rooms shouting 'Come on then, Adolf! Come and have a go if you think you're hard enough!' while his generals grabbed him by the arm and dragged him away from the map of Europe shouting, 'Leave it, Winston! He's not worth it, mate!'?

TIRED AND EMOTIONAL: BORIS YELTSIN, THE DRUNKEN PRESIDENT

No one ever said that Winston Churchill couldn't handle his drink, but there was one statesman who was regularly accused of being drunk while in charge of an entire country – a superpower in fact. Thankfully, Boris Yeltsin was President of

Russia for a relatively short period immediately following the thawing of the Cold War, because I hate to think what could have happened if he had been the boss during a nuclear stand-off. Yeltsin's exploits were often covered up at the time and only fully revealed years later.

In 1994, Yeltsin set off for Ireland to sit down with his opposite number, Taoiseach Albert Reynolds. Four days earlier, the thankfully sober President of the Russian Federation had addressed the United Nations in New York. He then visited Seattle and Washington before jetting home via a pit stop in Ireland. Perhaps he felt he'd earned a drink by then. Whatever the reason, when the President's jet reached Ireland, he didn't get off.

The Irish prime minister had actually cut a trip to Australia short once he learned that Yeltsin wanted to meet him in Ireland. The prospect of such an important visitor spurred the Irish into laying on a reception committee, which included thirty cars to take the guests to an official dinner at Dromoland Castle. An honour guard of a hundred soldiers stood by to salute Yeltsin's arrival. His plane was spotted by air traffic control, but instead of landing at Shannon, as expected, it began to circle the airport. It continued to do this for an hour, to the bemusement of the Irish contingent. Reynolds waited and waited.

Finally, the plane landed and the Irish prime minister went to meet Yeltsin – but he failed to emerge. An explanation was finally offered. The Russian President was ill. Reynolds offered sympathy and understanding. These things happen after all. He agreed to meet Yeltsin's deputy but requested the chance at least to board the plane, greet his poorly Russian counterpart and offer him a speedy recovery. The Russians were having none of that. Request denied. People all over the world drew their own conclusions, especially the Irish. Yeltsin was so drunk he could not get off the plane.

Later, Yeltsin claimed he was not ill after all, but certainly not drunk. No, he was just very tired and had fallen asleep and no one woke him. Heads would roll!

No one believed him.

With a typically wry sense of humour, the Irish adopted the phrase 'circling over the Shannon' to describe the condition of someone who is very drunk indeed.

Sadly, this was not an isolated incident. You can only imagine the level of security involving meetings between the Presidents of the United States and Russia. Weeks of advance planning, serious manpower and money – the stress levels of all concerned must be at their absolute peak. Imagine if anything went wrong: if you lost a president on your watch? So, the last thing security men in Washington would want is a Russian President who gets drunk, strips down to his underwear, and exits the White House without telling anyone, then flags down a cab on Pennsylvania Avenue so he can head into the city in search of … pizza.

If this sounds to you like a drunken, Slavic version of *Roman Holiday* – without Audrey Hepburn but with the actual Russian President just wanting to be normal for an evening – don't get too carried away. There is no evidence to indicate that Yeltsin remembered any of it the next day … but the following evening he went out and did it again! The second time was even worse, because he tried to exit the White House at a point where an alarmed guard standing there mistook him for a drunken intruder instead of a drunken statesman. Russian and US security men converged at this point and, somewhat miraculously, no one was actually shot dead in the resulting confusion.

Boris Yeltsin may have somehow achieved the rank of Russian President, but he never came close to attaining the title of Professor of Pintfulness.

HOW MUCH?
THE MOST EXPENSIVE BEER

The world's most expensive bottle of beer cost a phenomenal $16,000.

That was the sum paid at auction for a single bottle of Lowenbrau beer and there was nothing particularly special about either the bottle or its contents. It was just a normal beer.

The huge price it achieved was due to its history. The bottle was rescued, against all odds, from the wreckage of the downed airship *Hindenburg*, which famously burst into flames while attempting to dock in New Jersey on 6 May 1937, killing thirty-six of the ninety-seven passengers and crew on board.

The fact that this slightly fire-damaged bottle of beer is the most expensive ever, simply because it was in the vicinity of a sickening human tragedy as it unfolded, tells you quite a lot about mankind.

A SWIFT ONE:
THE FASTEST BEER DRINKER

Steven Petrosino from Pennsylvania holds the officially recognised world record for fastest beer drinking. In 1977, he chugged a litre of beer in just 1.3 seconds, gaining him a place in the *Guinness Book of World Records*. Fair play to him. It probably takes longer to pour beer down a sink.

NO SUCH THING AS A FREE LUNCH: THE PENNSYLVANIA BEER LAW

While on the subject of Pennsylvania ...

Offering a free lunch to your patrons was made illegal there in 1917 and remains so to the present day, the authorities being worried that giving away free sandwiches in bars would encourage workers to drink beer in their lunch hours. Perhaps they were concerned that productivity would go down as a result, or maybe they wouldn't return to work at all.

Some enterprising bar owners responded to the legislation by spinning it round and offering free beer with food, an imaginative but expensive way of putting up two fingers to authority or, as they might say in America, 'sticking it to the man'.

BAPTISED IN BEER:
YOU REALLY COULD BE

In the thirteenth century in Norway it was possible – even likely – that good, practising Catholics would insist their children were baptised in beer. This was a direct result of a water shortage in the affected region, but it was not an alternative that filled the Pope with enthusiasm.

In the Catholic Church, baptism is the first sacrament and you cannot receive any others if this one isn't performed correctly. According to doctrine, the minister must use water in the service. Beer might be a tempting substitute, in the absence of a ready supply of H_2O, but it unfortunately renders a baptism null and void.

In the end, Pope Gregory IX (1227–41) was forced to intervene. In a letter to Archbishop Sigurd of Nidaros, written in 1241, he felt compelled to spell out the obvious:

> Since as we have learned from your report, it sometimes happens because of the scarcity of water, that infants of your lands are baptised in beer, we reply to you in the tenor of those present that, since according to evangelical doctrine it is necessary 'to be reborn from water and the Holy Spirit' [John 3:5] they are not to be considered rightly baptised who are baptised in beer.

That's settled then. But I can't help feeling the Pope was being a bit of a spoilsport. Imagine if someone asked you whether you liked beer and you could actually reply 'Like it? I was bloody baptised in it!'

OKTOBERFEST:
7 MILLION LITRES OF BEER

It started with a kiss ... well, a wedding actually. The world-renowned Oktoberfest beer festival is an official celebration that began in 1810, to celebrate the nuptials of Crown Prince Ludwig of Bavaria and the Princess Therese of Saxony-Hildburghausen. That must have been some wedding!

The festivities, which mostly involved eating and drinking, went on for five days – there have been marriages that didn't last as long. The celebrations included a horse race, which proved so popular it was decided to stage it annually and continue with the eating and drinking. So far, Oktoberfest has been held 186 times, with a few postponements. There have been twenty-four occasions when there has been no Oktoberfest, and this can often be blamed on the outbreak of war: the Austro-Prussian War in 1866, the Franco-Prussian War of 1870, the First World War (1914–18) and the Second World War (1939–45) all temporarily put paid to the festivities. Two separate cholera epidemics, in 1854 and 1873, also put a damper on proceedings.

Oktoberfest is the largest beer festival in the world. You could guess from its name that it starts in October ... but it doesn't. Most of Oktoberfest actually occurs in *September*, with only the conclusion occurring in the first week of October. Why it isn't called Septemberfest remains a mystery.

More than 6 million people attend the festival outside Munich annually. It's held in a meadow named Theresienwiese, after Ludwig's bride, though most people call the place by its shortened name 'Wiesn'. Between them, these visitors drink 7 *million* litres of beer and munch their way through 500,000 chickens and 200,000 sausages. Guest are seated on long wooden benches in thirty tents – and when I say tents, I mean enormous marquees that are capable of seating several thousand people.

It is also the world's largest folk festival and there are fairground rides but frankly who cares? Surely this one is all about the beer.

If you like to blend in and wish to adopt local dress then you've come to the right place. Women can wear a dirndl, which is the traditional Bavarian outfit that includes a bodice, skirt and apron. If you can carry that off then you could end up looking like Heidi from *Where Eagles Dare*, as played by Ingrid Pitt and ...

Now, where was I? Sorry, lost my train of thought for a moment.

Oh yes, traditional costume! Men who are feeling very daring might like to wear lederhosen, the flattering leather breeches that ... ha! Seriously? You didn't actually believe I was going to suggest *voluntarily* donning lederhosen? No one – but *no one* – can carry that look off. At best, you'll end up looking like Benny Hill, and at worst? I don't even want to contemplate it. Leave the dressing up to the ladies and shameless locals and stick to the beer drinking.

The beer itself is local to Munich, comes in litre glasses and will set you back around a tenner a time, so make sure you are not short of funds.

With so many tents, people and beer, Oktoberfest always ends with a very long list of lost property items. One year, someone even lost a Dachshund by the name of Wasti. Imagine how drunk you would have to be to leave your dog behind.

A TOAST TO THE HAPPY COUPLE:
THE BRIDE-ALE PARTY

Many of you will have stayed in a bridal suite or been in a bridal party and become familiar with an entire industry that uses the word to extort money during the wedding planning process. Bridal showers, bridal hair, bridal dresses and bridal shoes all have something in common (aside from the fact that they cost a small fortune and are wedding related): they each have an historic link to beer.

The word bridal actually originates from 'bride ale'. In the Middle Ages, it was not uncommon for churches to hold special events involving beer, where music would be played and there would be dancing. Back then, the drinking of ale at a church function wasn't frowned upon because it was better for the box office at fundraising events, since people are far more likely to part with their money when they have had a few.

Occasions like these would see the brewing of 'church ale' or 'parish ale'. Weddings followed this pattern, with the making of bridal ale, which was given to guests who would then contribute towards funds raised for the newlywed couple to start their lives together. Centuries later, we still drink at weddings and give gifts to the happy couple.

ORWELL AND UTOPIA:
THE PERFECT PUB

According to George Orwell, the perfect pub has ten essential ingredients. The author of *1984* and *Animal Farm*, was famous for his dystopian views on the world and his damning critiques of the Stalinist system. He was less widely known for his far more utopian views on pubs.

In 1946, he wrote a piece for **the** *Evening Standard* about the attributes of an ideal pub, the sadly fictional 'Moon Under Water'. We might not all agree on every one of these, but a lot of them could feature in the perfect modern-day pub.

1. It should have Victorian fittings.
2. Games should only be allowed in the public bar, so you can walk freely in other bars while avoiding flying darts.
3. No music should be played either from the radio or piano, so it is quiet enough to talk.
4. Tobacco and cigarettes are on sale [this was half a century before the indoor smoking ban that would have horrified Orwell] and stamps and aspirins [handy for that hangover the next day!] should be sold.
5. A snack counter would sell liver-sausage sandwiches, mussels, cheese, and pickles, with large biscuits.
6. Draft stout should be served in a pewter pot.
7. Bar staff know the names of their customers and take an interest in them.

8. A good solid lunch is available upstairs, consisting of a cut off the joint, vegetables and a boiled jam roll – all for no more than three shillings.
9. They are particular about their drinking vessels and never serve beer in a handle-less glass.
10. There's a large beer garden out back for the family to use and not just dad going to the pub on his own [quite an enlightened view from a male writing in 1946].

Sadly for Orwell, he only ever found a pub that had eight out of the ten of his most favoured features. He concludes: 'If anyone knows of a pub that has draught stout, open fires, cheap meals, a garden, motherly barmaids and no radio, I should be glad to hear of it.'

And so would I.

BEERY MYTHS AND LEGENDS

In mythology and legend there are a number of characters who have a special association with beer. Here are some whose names you can slip into casual conversation, so you can impress your friends and charm girls with your detailed knowledge of the saints and gods of Pintfulness.

I'm joking of course; no one will give a shit, least of all women.

THE GODDESS OF BEER

You didn't know there was a goddess of beer? There is and her name is Ninkasi. She came from quite a lineage too: Ninkasi's mother was the high priestess for the temple of the goddess of procreation. What a family!

This must have made Ninkasi pretty popular with the male gods. I mean, who wouldn't want to marry Ninkasi, assuming she was fun to be with and not entirely unpleasing on the eye? Anyone who gets to become the goddess of beer must surely have been decent company or they would have been underqualified for the job. This is the immortals' equivalent of marrying a lass whose father owns a brewery. Talk about a win-win.

The ancient Sumerian poem 'A Hymn to Ninkasi' isn't actually a hymn at all. It's a step-by-step recipe for beer, designed to be handed down verbally from generation to generation, at a time when written records of any kind were almost non-existent.

Imagine getting the kids to learn a hymn to a goddess, so that they and their children's children would one day know how to make beer. Genius.

THE PATRON SAINT OF BREWERS ...
AND ALL OF HIS MATES

Being the patron saint of brewers would be a popular position, wouldn't it? You can just imagine all the saints in the room when everything is being handed out: 'Okay then, who wants to be the patron saint of STDs? No one? Oh, come on. Well, what about the patron saint of lost causes? No? Okay then, who wants to be the patron saint of brewers? Seriously? Put your hands down. You can't *all* be the patron saint of brewers, for f**k's sake!'

That's how it must have gone, which would explain why a quest to find the patron saint of brewers yields not one but half a dozen answers.

St Nicholas: The Patron Saint of Brewers (Candidate 1)

One of the main candidates for the patron saint of brewers is St Nicholas, he of Santa Claus fame. If you ever wondered why the most recognisable image we have of Santa Claus is of a big guy with an enormous belly, bright red face and jovial gleam in his eye, then look no further than that fact for your answer. Now you've seen it, you can't unsee the obvious. He's a *massive* drinker. It would also explain how he is able to consume so much beer, wine and sherry left out for him on Christmas Eve, yet still somehow function and give everyone the right presents. Fair play to the man.

I always used to think that St Nick had it pretty cushy, since he only seemed to work one night a year, but it turns out he was a very busy lad indeed. As well as brewers, he is also the patron saint of archers, merchants, pawnbrokers, students, thieves, sailors, and – not that surprisingly in his present-giving role – children.

That is one hell of a portfolio, and a pretty full-on 24–7 series of jobs and responsibilities. No wonder the poor bugger had a drink problem.

St Boniface: The Patron Saint of Brewers (Candidate 2)

While visiting a friend in Dublin, I was amused when I heard her say a quiet prayer under her breath as she pulled into a parking spot in a multistorey car park. It wasn't the prayer as such that made me smile; like many people from the Emerald Isle, she was Catholic and reasonably devout. The amusing bit was the explanation that followed: 'My mother always said that when you find a space you should say a prayer to St Boniface, the patron saint of parking.'

The patron saint of *parking*? I and my fellow passengers cracked up. I had always assumed that to be the patron saint of something it had to be a suitably ancient thing, like seafaring or winemaking, but no, parking apparently is a matter of such importance that it has been allocated a saint by the Catholic Church. Don't feel too bad for St Boniface though, because he wasn't just burdened with every Catholic who can't find a spot to park in. He was also the patron saint of tailors and of Germany – but he is perhaps best known as the patron saint of brewers. So, if you are a German brewer looking for a parking spot outside a tailor's, then Boniface will be smiling down on you.

While on the subject of patron saints there are many other unusual ones:

St Genesius is the patron saint of comedians.

St Fiacre is the patron saint of people with STDs (I wasn't joking about that. I guess they need one, but the poor bastard).

St Drogo is the patron saint of unattractive people. You have to feel sorry for them, but at least they have their own saint.

And if you ever overindulge and blame St Boniface for your condition the next morning, then how about saying a quick prayer to St Bibiana, who is, would you believe, the patron saint of hangovers.

YOU OWE ME A PINT:
PAYING IN BEER

If the Sumerians win the title of earliest recorded brewers, then it was the Egyptians who actually perfected the art. Their beer was smoother and lighter and easily poured into a glass. In effect they made what has been acknowledged as the first beer and it was primarily brewed by women in the home, which is probably why the Egyptians, like the Sumerians, had a female goddess of beer and not a male god. Their goddess was called Tenenet. Beer was used in religious festivals and offered to the souls of the dead.

The Egyptians took brewing so seriously they even used beer as a form of currency: pyramid workers received a gallon of beer a day, receiving this ration in three servings throughout the day.

Sadly, all of that history and brewing expertise was lost when the popularity of Islam outlawed the drinking of beer in Egypt around AD 800.

THE LONG AND THE SHORT OF IT: THE LONGEST AND SHORTEST PUB NAMES

If you're going to run a pub, it's probably quite important to give it a catchy name so it always stays in the mind of your customers. That was probably the traditional thinking behind common names such as The Red Lion and The Dun Cow. How then can you explain the origin of the longest pub name in Britain? How could you remember or confidently recommend a watering hole called The Old Thirteenth Cheshire Astley Volunteer Rifleman Corps Inn, unless, of course, you are a member of the (probably long defunct) 13th Cheshire Astley Volunteer Rifleman Corps?

I suppose tradition is a good thing and there is probably some mileage in having the record-holding name. It might inspire a bit of beer-tourism from the kind of person who gets themselves photographed beside the sign for the Welsh town of Llanfairpwllgwyngyllgogerychwyrndrobwllllantysiliogogogoch.

There is a downside to running the pub with the longest name, however. Its most recent owners commissioned a new sign and had to pay the signwriter by the letter. Since there are fifty-five of them in the pub's name, it was pretty expensive.

And so, to the shortest pub name in Britain. That distinction goes to the Q Inn, which by a strange coincidence is not only also in Stalybridge, but a mere two doors along from The Old Thirteenth Cheshire Astley Volunteer Rifleman Corps Inn. If you so desire, you can have a pint in the pub with the longest name then one in the pub with the shortest name, one after the other, without putting yourself to any trouble at all.

The landlord of the Q Inn will most likely try to convince you that his pub is better, because size is not important.

BEER BRICKS

In the 1960s, brewing heir Albert Heineken had an idea that he hoped would transform housing in impoverished parts of the world. The notion came to him while he was on a trip to the Caribbean. The brewery CEO was well ahead of his time, in that the amount of discarded rubbish he saw on the beaches actually bothered him, especially when it included used bottles from his own brewery. He also cared more about the lack of housing for poor people than your average rich person.

Albert's big idea to help the world was to create a beer bottle durable enough to be used as a house brick once it was empty. The 'WOBO' (**wo**rld **bo**ttle) was designed by Dutch architect John Habraken. Around 100,000 of these thick, rectangular-shaped blocks of glass were produced, and they locked together like Lego. Sadly, they never really caught on, and Albert failed to fulfil his ambitions to end housing shortages in the developing world – but a small, green glasshouse near to his home was built out of them and looks amazing.

PILGRIM'S PROGRESS:
PLYMOUTH ROCK

In 1620, the Pilgrim Fathers landed at Plymouth Rock and founded America (if you discount the obvious fact that Native Americans had been there for many, *many* years already). But why did they pick that spot, instead of their original intended destination of the already established English colony of Virginia?

The captain of the *Mayflower* had a difficult decision to make. The ship was still more than 200 nautical miles from Virginia and sailing in treacherous conditions – but that wasn't uppermost in Christopher Jones' mind.

The hundred Puritans he was carrying to the new world had survived religious persecution in their homeland, then endured no fewer than sixty-four days at sea in cramped conditions. They were tough and resilient people, but the one thing they apparently could not bear was a shortage of beer. The ship was running out and the captain knew exactly what that meant.

It wasn't that the Puritans were all massive ale heads who couldn't cope if they weren't getting pissed together every night. With fresh water in short supply and often insanitary, beer was required to provide the ship's crew and passengers with something drinkable that would give them nutrition and hopefully not kill them in the process. When it started to run low, the decision became no decision at all. Captain Jones cut the journey short and set the Pilgrim Fathers down on Plymouth Rock instead. History was made on that spot – and all because of beer.

WILLIAM SHAKESBEER:
SHAKESPEARE'S BEERY DEMISE
AND HIS THOUGHTS ON ALE

We'll teach you to drink deep ere you depart.

That's Hamlet speaking to his friend Horatio, who has just arrived at Elsinore. They are possibly the most sensible words the confused Prince of Denmark utters during the entire eponymous play that centres around his tortured existence. Even Hamlet knew the value of a pint with a mate, and logic dictates that his creator, William Shakespeare, our finest-ever dramatist, did too. Only a man who truly understood pubs (alehouses) could have created a man like Falstaff. Shakespeare did not waste his wild youth: he wrote about it. Mentions of beer, ale and wine appear frequently throughout his plays. Here are just a few of his wise words:

Come, gentlemen, I hope we shall drink down all unkindness.
The Merry Wives of Windsor, Act 1, Scene 1

What better way to resolve a quarrel before it even starts than by having a drink together?

I have very poor and unhappy brains for drinking. I could well wish courtesy would invent some other custom of entertainment.

Othello, Act 2, Scene 3

Othello was a lightweight, wasn't he? He has no head for booze, never understands the art of Pintfulness, and subsequently takes life far too seriously. Shakespeare uses this to make us immediately suspicious of him, I reckon. He's doesn't like a beer, so he must be a wrong 'un, eh? If only Othello had been able to have the occasional sip of ale he might have chilled out, instead of believing that his wife Desdemona was cheating on him with Cassio. Then he might not have strangled her and killed himself.

This is what comes of being teetotal.

> Would I were in an alehouse in London. I would give all my fame for a pot of ale and safety.
>
> *Henry V*, Act 3, Scene 2

I wish I was in a pub and not about to be killed in a battle.

> Do you think because you are virtuous, that there shall be no more cakes and ale?
>
> *Twelfth Night*, Act 2, Scene 3

No more good living? You're kidding, right?

> I drink to the general joy of the whole table.
>
> *Macbeth*, Act 3, Scene 4

Before killing them all? This *is* Macbeth, after all.

Good company, good wine, good welcome can make good people.

Henry VIII, Act 1, Scene 4

Explains Henry VIII, who had two of his own wives executed.

It is reported that Shakespeare died following a particularly legendary night out with fellow playwright Ben Jonson and the poet Michael Drayton. It must have been a bloody riotous one: only a month earlier he had described himself as being in 'perfect health' while writing his will.

This salutary tale should not be taken as a reason to avoid Pintfulness, however. We've all had one too many at some point in our lives, but we are unlikely to catch a fever and die as a result of it.

Besides, the average life expectancy back then was just 42, so Shakespeare outlived that by a decade – or, to put it another way, he lived nearly 20 per cent longer than his compatriots. He was into the equivalent of time added on for stoppages by this stage and went out with a bang not a whimper. What better way to end your life than after a night of spectacular drinking with close friends? It's surely the way he would have wanted it. Me too, now that I come to mention it.

MAGICAL ALCHEMY:
THE BREWING PROCESS

The creation of beer is a form of heavenly alchemy so magical that it might lead you to believe there actually is a God. You might also conclude that he is up there somewhere looking down on us and that his intentions for the human race are benign.

When you follow any recipe, the first thing you need to do is assemble all of your ingredients.

Water: You were expecting this one, right? More than 90 per cent of that beer in your glass is made up of water. If you want to brew beer, you are going to need a good source of the old H_2O.

Not just any water will do either. The type you use is so important that the town of Burton-on-Trent became a centre for brewing because water from its local river was perfect for the brewing process. At one point, the output of this market town, with a population of just over 70,000, amounted to as much as *25 per cent* of the UK's beer production. This was all based on the composition of the water supply from the River Trent, the third-longest river in the country, which passed through it and happened to be naturally high in sulphur. This happy accident of nature gave Burton a huge industry and a reputation for beer making that it is still synonymous with. Local names like Bass, Worthingtons and Ind Coope are equally well known.

This water source was so important to the quality of the beer that nowadays the effects of it are (rather disappointingly) artificially reproduced by beer makers in a process known as 'Burtonisation'. This is done with the addition of gypsum, a sulphate mineral more commonly used as a fertiliser.

This robbing of the town's unique selling point, along with an increase in taxes and the popularity of lager, meant a slow but steady decline of Burton as a brewing centre.

Hops: As well as being a natural preservative, it is hops that add bitterness and flavour to your beer.

Cereals: When I say cereals, I am not talking about Corn Flakes or Coco Pops. This is the kind of cereal farmers grow and harvest before it finds its way into the bread we eat. The most commonly used cereal in the brewing process is malted barley, which provides a source of starch and can be converted into sugars and then alcohol (ethanol).

Yeast: Yeast is responsible for the fermentation of the beer, taking the sugars extracted from the grains and turning them into alcohol. Yeast can also influence the flavour of the beer.

Mix all of that together in the right quantities for the requisite amount of time and you end up with beer. Lovely beer.

STRANGE BREWS

DON'T GET FRUITY

Originating in Belgium, fruit beers have inexplicably reached these shores of late and gained in popularity. Quite how this has happened is beyond me, since no true Professor of Pintfulness would ever stoop so low as to drink a beer that listed strawberries as one of its main ingredients, even on the very hottest of summer days.

In Belgium, however, they have no shame, so they've been combining fruit with sour ales for years, to create reasonably well-known beers. These have unappealing names such as 'Lactose & Blueberry Berliner Weisse' or 'Key Lime Tau', which its own brewers will tell you is a 'kettle-soured, lactose infused golden ale brewed with fresh lime zest and lemon grass', designed to taste like key lime pie. I mean, good luck to them and everything but I want my beer to taste of *beer*, not tiramisu or banoffee pie. They think they are brewing beer, but what they have actually succeeded in making is dessert in liquid form.

Thankfully there is enough of this nonsense around without having to resort to the importation of the worst of the worst: banana beer. Yes, banana beer! I get that in countries where there is a proliferation of bananas, it might be tempting to turn the surplus into beer, but is that any reason to inflict it on the rest of the world? I think not.

Strawberry, raspberry, grapefruit, cherry, orange, banana and mango beer – these are all things that exist.

They really shouldn't.

End of.

CHOCOLATE BEER

Don't even get me started.

Chocolate is a fine thing and so is beer, but they should never be combined. This only leads to the ruination of both items.

SUN ABOVE THE YARD ARM:
BEER O'CLOCK

Work is over, so what the hell are we still doing here?

When someone worries that it might be too early for a drink, an old-fashioned response is to state that 'The sun is over the yard arm somewhere in the world', which is a lovely idea and a damn fine excuse to break out the booze.

A more modern query might be 'is it beer o'clock yet?' This does of course beg the question: when exactly is beer o'clock and is it an official time? It could be argued that more or less *any* time could be beer o'clock, depending on the circumstances. I have drunk a pint of beer at 7.00 a.m. before – this is not a regular occurrence nor was it a normal sort of day, I hasten to add. I was about to board a flight from Heathrow to Riga for a very messy stag do, so it seemed an appropriate time for us all to begin drinking.

Lunchtime drinking is also allowed, of course, and should be encouraged, but not every day. However, the use of the phrase beer o'clock should really be reserved for the end of a long and trying workday that has left everyone with frazzled nerves and a less-than-jovial disposition. In this instance, it is perfectly acceptable to ask, rhetorically and pleadingly, 'Is it beer o'clock yet?' at any time after 5.00 p.m. If said with enough conviction, the phrase can even lead to the formation of a posse, which will then head en masse to the nearest pub to make the end of the miserable day more palatable for all.

LIVING LIKE A MONK:
TRAPPIST BREWING

That old phrase 'living like a monk' does kind of imply that the lifestyle is pretty boring. For starters, there are no women around, in theory at least (though it is highly likely that many monks throughout history ignored this rule in practice; some even had wives!).

But what attracted them to a life of prayer and relative solitude in the first place?

Most people assume it was all about worshipping God – and yes, that was a fairly major factor, in a world where belief in a higher Christian deity was almost universal. People gave money to the church, so it was usual for monks to have enough to feed themselves. This wasn't always the case in the wider world, where individuals were more susceptible to the effects of food shortages caused by crop failures.

Monks were also less likely to be set upon by hostile forces. Most people, even very bad ones, hesitated to attack religious men, because they worried about the divine retribution that might befall them from a vengeful God, in this life or the next. That held true right up to the point when the Vikings, who had no belief in or fear of God, attacked Lindisfarne in AD 793 and found the monastery there wholly unprotected. They promptly slaughtered or enslaved all of the monks. But still, generally speaking, monks were safer and better off than most people and it stayed that way for centuries.

But it could, perhaps, have been the plentiful rations of beer. It was considered quite normal for monks to brew their own, a practice which continues to this day in mainland Europe. Trappist (Cistercian) monks in particular were expected to earn their living, which they did by producing goods such as beer.

In England, this lifestyle came to an abrupt end when Henry VIII cast envious eyes at monastic land and closed the monasteries down so he could keep their wealth for himself. The brewing of Trappist beer was then left to monks operating in Europe. There are still eight monasteries – one Dutch, one German and six Belgian – that are allowed to brew beer using the term Trappist. They formed the International Trappist Association in 1997 and even have their own logo, which can only be used on products actually produced in Trappist monasteries, to prevent others from cashing in on the term.

In 2018, Mount St Bernard monastery in the Midlands made history. Following a gap of several hundred years, the practice of brewing beer in an English monastery finally reappeared.

A Cistercian abbey since 1835, Mount St Bernard always relied on a dairy farm for its income, but this was closed when it became uneconomic. They were then left with the problem of what to replace it with, to provide much needed revenue. Following the example of Cistercian monasteries in Belgium, they decided to make a craft beer, but were determined it would not be a mere copy of the Belgian Trappist ales that had already flooded the market. Instead, their beer has a distinctly English taste. They used English barley, hops and yeast to make a beer called 'Tynt Meadow'.

It's apparently very good. Why not try some, if you want to 'live like a monk'?

A BEER BY ANY OTHER NAME
WOULD TASTE AS SWEET:
THE UNIVERSAL LANGUAGE OF BEER

It is a testimony to the appeal of beer and the long-standing popularity of Pintfulness that the word itself is instantly recognisable almost anywhere in the world, up there alongside 'Okay' and 'Coca-Cola'.

The word 'beer' comes from the Latin *bibere*, which means 'to drink' – proving once again that it dates back a very long way.

A huge number of countries use the word 'beer', even if the spelling differs slightly from place to place. Below I have listed thirty-five of them that use a variation on the word. Following my extensive research, it would appear that around 50 per cent of countries call a beer a beer.

In Spain, Portugal and Latin America, beer is known as *cerveza*. In Eastern Europe it's *pivo* or something similar. For pretty much the rest of the world you can utter the word 'beer' and you'll be fine.

Now that you are armed with this vital knowledge there is simply no excuse for shouting '*Dos* lagers!' at the top of your voice at unfortunate Spanish barmen.

For the subtle differences in spelling of the almost universal word 'beer', check out the nations below:

Afrikaans	*bier*	Indonesian	*bir*
Albanian	*birrë*	Interlingua	*bira*
Arabic	*beereh*	Irish (Gaeilge)	*beoir*
Bengali	*beer*	Italian	*birra*
Breton	*bier*	Japanese	*biiru*
Bulgarian	*bira*	Kurdish	*bîre*
Dutch	*bier*	Malay	*bir*
English	*beer*	Neo	*biro*
Esperanto	*biero*	Nepali	*biyar*
Flemish	*bier*	Romanian	*bere*
French	*bière*	Swahili	*bia*
Frisian	*bier*	Thai	*bia*
German	*bier*	Turkish	*bira*
Hebrew	*beera*	Vietnamese	*bia*
Hindi	*beer*	Volapük	*bil*
Icelandic	*bjór*	Yiddish	*bir*
Ido	*biro*		

Of course, if all else fails and you find yourself in a far-flung corner of the globe where the people converse in a language or dialect so obscure they don't understand the word **'beer'** in any of its forms, simply hold your hand out in front of you with the fingers curled inwards, as if cradling a pint, then raise that imaginary glass and tilt it so it appears you are supping an alcoholic beverage. They'll get the message.

INTERNATIONAL BEER DAY

You didn't realise there was an International Beer Day? Seriously, haven't you been paying attention? These days, there is an international day for virtually everything, including:

Sleep: 3 January Encouraging you to sleep in late, possibly even for the entire day.
National Unicorn Day: 7 April Yes, really.
Wonderful Weirdos Day: 9 September Self-explanatory, surely.

There is even an 'Ice Cream for Breakfast' day, on the first Saturday in February. So is it any wonder someone did it for beer? But are they a Professor of Pintfulness or a ruthless marketeer exploiting the gullibility of consumers? You can be the judge.

Like more or less everything designed to get people to buy more of something, it originated in the home of unfettered capitalism: the United States of America. It started in Santa Cruz, California, and is celebrated annually on the first Friday in August. International Beer Day was the brainchild of Jesse Avshalomov, who, *quelle surprise*, works in marketing.

In the dozen years since it began, International Beer Day has spread to eighty countries. Apparently, the 'concept' (a marketing word if ever I heard one) is to meet friends and drink beer with them, while celebrating the makers and servers of beers and giving the whole thing an international slant by drinking beers from different parts of the world. My initial observation is why would you need an official day to do this? Doesn't it exist already and isn't it simply called 'Saturday'?

It is also meant to encourage people to give the gift of beer or, to put it another way, get a round in. You can gather that I am unconvinced and more than a little underwhelmed by International Beer Day, but I am clearly in the minority. Take a quick glance at the list of countries that now celebrate it:

Argentina
Armenia
Australia
Austria
Belgium
Brazil
Bulgaria
Canada
Colombia
Costa Rica
El Salvador
England
France
Greece
Honduras
Hong Kong
Hungary
India
Ireland
Israel
Italy
Japan
Latvia

Lebanon
Lithuania
Luxembourg
Macedonia
Malaysia
Mexico
New Zealand
Nicaragua
Norway
Peru
Poland
Portugal
Puerto Rico
Romania
Scotland
Serbia
Singapore
Slovakia
Slovenia
South Africa
Spain
Sri Lanka
Sweden

Thailand

The Philippines

Turkey

Uganda

Ukraine

United Arab Emirates

United States

Uruguay

Vanuatu

Venezuela

So, it looks like there is only one thing for it: If you can't beat them, join them, and raise a glass of beer or two on International Beer Day!

99 BOTTLES OF BEER ON THE WALL:
THE INVENTION OF THE BEER BOTTLE

Bottled beer has been around for a long time; more than 400 years in fact.

A parish priest called Alexander Howell is said to have invented it, when he poured some ale from a keg in his home into a bottle, then went fishing in his native Hertfordshire and unintentionally left the bottle behind on the riverbank. He went back the next day and found that the beer had undergone a secondary fermentation inside the sealed bottle.

Congrats, Alexander, you accidentally invented a gassy, bottled beer. It sounds like a good story, but there is no concrete evidence to suggest it is actually true or that this then led to any form of commercialised beer bottling, which only happened a couple of centuries later in the late 1800s.

Before that, the earliest beer bottles were made from iron moulds and looked not dissimilar to the bottles we drink from today. They were a bit of a luxury then and unstable, because the glass wasn't always strong enough to cope with the chemical reaction of the beer inside it, leaving it liable to explode under the wrong conditions.

In the 1870s Whitbread built a large bottling plant that required a hundred workers to only do one very important task: hammer in the corks used to keep the beer in the bottles. Back then, beer drinkers had to open them like wine bottles, with a corkscrew, until Henry Barrett invented the screw top in the same decade.

Then, in 1892, an American, William Painter, invented the still-familiar 'crown cork' seal that you can snick from the top of the bottle with a conventional opener even now.

And if that is not enough beer-bottle trivia for you for one day, here's another snippet. A collector of beer bottles or their labels is a 'labeorphilist'. I suppose then that someone who does not appreciate a good bottle of beer is a 'labeorphilistine' or possibly even a 'labeorphilistein'?

No? Okay, I'll get my coat.

IT'S IN THE CAN:
THE INVENTION OF THE BEER CAN

As Prohibition came to an end, a new invention brought something of a revolution to the world of beer.

The aptly named American Can Company managed to develop a workable can that could contain beer without explosive consequences. They had to wait fourteen months for a brewing company brave enough to take up their new invention and try it on members of the public. In Newark, New Jersey, the Gottfried Krueger Brewing Company decided to give it a go.

On 24 January 1935 in Richmond, Virginia, USA, history was made, when 2,000 cans filled with Krueger's Finest Beer and Krueger's Cream Ale were distributed to some of the brewery's most loyal customers.

It is recorded that 91 per cent of those who tried the new canned beer approved of it and 85 per cent preferred it to bottled beer, deeming it closer to the taste of the draft version. Beer in cans was considered a good thing by a sizeable majority and it was clearly here to stay. Canned beer became something of a craze; big competitors began to get in on the act and more than 200 million cans were sold by the end of the year. The outbreak of the Second World War made them even more popular because they were more robust than bottles, could be transported more easily, and were more likely to survive a journey oversees to thirsty troops.

Initially beer cans had a flat top. A cone top was developed later, but you had to jump forward almost thirty years to 1963 for the real revolution, which came with the tab top can and the development of the ring pull. All you now needed to open a can of beer was your finger and millions of ring-pull cans have been consumed since that day, often by sports-loving armchair fans who prefer the company of the TV to watching the game down the pub.

Word of this new American invention, the beer can, soon reached Europe and enterprising folks tried to imitate it. The Felinfoel Brewery in Llanelli, Carmarthenshire, became the first in the UK to follow this new trend but they couldn't just import the American technology and start putting British beer into it. There was a particular problem to overcome first: our beer reacted badly to the tin, which left a metallic taste. Felinfoel fretted over this for some time before finding a solution. They put a wax coating on the inside of their can and the metallic taste was gone. Canned beer in the UK then proved just as popular as it had done in the States.

ONE FOR MY HOMIES:
POURING ONE OUT

The practice of pouring a drink onto the ground to honour the memory of a loved one is an incredibly old one. Known as a libation, it didn't have to be an alcoholic liquid, but the use of wine or beer was more common than mere water.

The custom started in Ancient Egypt, where it was offered to both ancestors and gods; continued in Ancient Greece, where it became a common religious practice; and was adopted in Roman times, as part of funeral rites, as well as animal sacrifice.

Thanks to gangsta rappers 'tipping to a dead homie', the practice is still widely adopted in the USA, where beer from 40oz bottles is poured for a fallen friend. True dat.

VALHALLA – KIND OF:
THE VIKING BEER HALL

A 1,100-year-old Viking 'beer hall' has been discovered in Scotland. And people say they weren't civilised.

Sigurd, a twelfth-century Viking earl, built a stone building for him and his men to sit in and drink beer while they discussed the day's pillaging and plunder.

What is described as 'a large Norse hall' was discovered during excavations by a team of archaeologists and students from the University of the Highlands and Islands Archaeology Institute. They had been digging up an old farmstead at Skaill, on the island of Rousay, Orkney.

The discovery of the drinking hall must have been something of a bonus for the students, because their original brief was to dig up a bunch of middens at the same location. For those of you unfamiliar with the word 'midden', it's basically a toilet, though its actual meaning is a dunghill or refuse heap – but that 'refuse' contained human excrement. If you are wondering why the Archaeology department decided to spend years excavating middens, there is a helpful explanation on the college's website:

> We have recovered a millennia of middens, which will allow us an unparalleled opportunity to look at changing dietary traditions, farming and fishing practices from the Norse period up until the 19th century.

So, there you have it. They were examining ancient poo.

I suspect the discovery of the beer hall will cause far more excitement than the middens, and I do wonder if the college should perhaps take the old advice that if you're already in the shit, you should probably stop digging.

IT AIN'T HEAVY:
A PINT OF HEAVY PLEASE

In Scotland it is not uncommon to refer to a glass of bitter as 'a pint of heavy'. This is another phrase with long-standing historical meaning; it's actually a reference to something way less popular than beer: taxes.

Back in the eighteenth century, beers were divided into tax bands depending on their strength. Scots are referring, unknowingly in most cases, to the cost of a hogshead of ale. A hogshead contains 64 gallons of beer and the tax on it was sixty shillings for beer under 3.5 per cent ABV (known as 'light')' seventy shillings if it was between 3.5 and 4 per cent (described as 'heavy'); eighty shillings when between 4 and 5.5 per cent (also referred to as 'heavy' or 'export'); and ninety shillings if over 5.5 per cent (known as 'wee heavy').

Since the majority of commercially produced beer these days falls into the 'heavy' category, people have been asking for a pint of heavy in Scotland for so many years that the origin of this phrase has been lost in time. Until today that is. Now you know it.

A GOOD SERVANT
BUT A POOR MASTER:
THE AVOIDANCE OF ADDICTION

Beer is a good servant but a poor master. Surely that is an adage we can all live by. Many of us are aware of the evils of drink and the adverse effects of booze on our health, wealth and wisdom if taken to excess.

Less well documented are the evils of sobriety, but the columnist Christopher Hitchens did a pretty good job in summing them up:

> It has been said that alcohol is a good servant and a bad master. Nice try. The plain fact is that it makes other people, and indeed life itself, a good deal less boring.

He does have a point.

THE RULES OF THE BAR

THE LOST ART OF PINTFULNESS

In my day (it's still my day but I'm probably older and wiser than you, so I'm allowed to talk down to you like this, possibly while wedging my thumbs under the elasticated straps of a sturdy pair of braces) we were taught what it was to be a bloke, and this always involved Pintfulness.

My grandfather took my own dad for his first pint when he was still underage (17) and the only shock involved in this time-honoured process was the price. It had gone up to eleven pence that day (this was 1957) and grandfather was appalled – however, he stopped just short of stating that he would never drink there again, because he knew better than that.

He also, presumably, taught my dad the etiquette of the pub: a series of unwritten rules that we shall cover here for those many souls unfortunate enough not to have been educated by their parents, and therefore unaware that there are some things you just do not do in a hostelry.

Everyone should know the rules of pub drinking. They should be on the national curriculum and taught in school instead of something no one really needs, like Religious Studies.

Like I said, these rules are not written down – which is fine if you are a Professor of Pintfulness, with years of experience behind you, but what if you are an apprentice drinker or millennial who hasn't spent enough time wasting your youth in bars?

Have no fear. Read on and become enlightened.

THE SANCTITY OF QUEUING

Re: pushing in. Don't do it, ever, even on a Saturday night when the bar is packed. Yes, you've been waiting ages and your mates are all in the corner having a right laugh, while you stand there helplessly clutching actual cash in your hand as a none-too-subtle hint to the bar staff that you have not yet been served, nor are you being looked after by one of their colleagues. When people push in ahead of you at this point, you might seriously contemplate homicide and later reflect that it is just as well we are not allowed to carry concealed firearms in this country.

In a quieter pub, with only a few people waiting, pushing in is an even more heinous sin. There's no bloody excuse for it. How much of a hurry can you possibly be in? Bar staff with actual cojones will intervene to ensure the right person is served next, but inexperienced or gutless ones will resort to a general proclamation involving the words 'Who's next please?', while blinking into the near distance and pretending they don't really know. This is copping out entirely and places the onus right back on you, or the person next to you, to say 'This gent/lady here' (be careful not to call a gent a lady or, possibly even worse, a lady a gent at this point).

Do the right thing here. You may even want to take a step backwards to acknowledge your less favourable place in the queue. The bar staff will be grateful for the clarification. The recipient of your largesse will offer their thanks and be glad that there is at least some chivalry left in the world. If they don't thank you at this point then they have broken one of the rules of the pub, and should probably be asked to leave right there and then.

THANK YOU FOR YOUR SERVICE

You will never be a Professor of Pintfulness if you are unsure how to treat bar staff. The answer is, of course, with the utmost respect at all times.

These underpaid, overworked artisans of pub craft have to tolerate the presence of members of the general public in their workplace. 'Just like everyone else who works in retail!' I hear you cry. Well, no. The crucial difference between their world and the working environment endured in Sainsbury's or John Lewis is that their customers have been drinking actual alcoholic beverages, which makes them worse – sometimes far, *far* worse – than sober ones.

Bar staff have to deal with drunk, aggressive, boring, belligerent, argumentative, self-opinionated halfwits on a daily basis. They work long, unsociable hours, while most people are either at home putting their feet up or out in pubs with their friends annoying bar staff. These facts alone should tell you that you should be incredibly courteous when dealing with the poor buggers.

I have been a drinker and proponent of Pintfulness for many a long year, but have also seen the pub from the other side of the tracks; having worked as a barman throughout my college years and beyond them. I was even full time as a barman for a year. This left me with the considered opinion that everyone should be made to work in a pub for at least six months, so they can see just how appalling other people can be and learn the value of good manners in the process. It would be a kind of national service, in which politeness would be instilled in people, instead of the ability to bayonet someone.

Bar staff should *never* be assailed; shouted at; sworn at; berated; cajoled; abused; whistled at (an absolutely abhorrent crime, for which a minimum six-month ban should be the automatic punishment); or, worst of all, have fingers clicked at them, as if they are your servants or slave. They are people, which sounds obvious to most of us, but you would be surprised by how many people seem to forget this.

THINGS NOT TO SAY TO BAR STAFF

'Cheer up, it'll soon be the weekend!'

Thanks, mate, I'll be doing two thirteen-hour split shifts then, and the place will be rammed with pricks like you – but cheers for reminding me of that.

'How much?!'

Let's be clear here. I don't own the place. I'm employed on minimum wage, I don't set the price of the beer and will not be getting a share of the profits. If you don't like the prices in here, buy a six pack of Tennent's Super from Asda instead and go and drink it under a bridge somewhere.

YOU DON'T OWN HER

Possibly the only thing more awkward than being a barman with a persistently annoying customer is being a barmaid with one (am I still allowed to use that insanely old-fashioned word? Probably not, so instead I'll go for bar staff of the female gender. God, I'm so woke).

For some reason there are (thankfully a minority of) men who seem to think they own female bar staff, simply because they are buying drinks the unfortunate lass is paid to provide. As 99 per cent of men thankfully know, this is not the case. Just because she has to speak to you during the transaction while beer and payment change hands, this does not give you the right to comment on her appearance, mood or disposition, while calling her love or darling. Similarly, you should refrain from telling her to 'cheer up' or 'smile'. Nowhere in her employment contract does it say that she has to smile at leering saddos – and that, my friend, means you, if you are thick-skinned enough to demand this.

CALLED TO THE BAR: APPRENTICE DRINKING

I know I am one of those old gits who keeps looking back on their childhood and saying 'in my day', but ...

In my day, when you were a kid the pub had a certain mystique to it. You weren't generally allowed in them; at least, not the proper drinking places that only provided food as a bit of an afterthought and served pints to a largely male clientele. You would look forward to the days when you were old enough to finally darken the doors of a pub and get served actual alcohol by bar staff who wouldn't immediately kick you out. Being brought up in the north-east and coming of age during an era when ID was unheard of (the early eighties, since you ask), this happened a little earlier than the legally permitted time. Most of my mates started around the same age as me: 16.

Oddly enough, the first alcoholic drink I ever bought was at a welcome disco for new sixth formers that had been organised by teachers. Yes, the first beer I ever drank in a pub was laid on by my school. These days heads would roll, the headteacher would be fired, and there would be dark mutterings about the state-sponsored depravity of underage drinking. At the time I didn't give it much thought, except for planning what I should ask for as I walked to the pub. Me and my mate had a lengthy discussion about what we should order. The problem was that a soft drink, as well as being unappealing to us, would mark us out as mere children, instead of the less-than-strapping 'men' we were, now that we had passed our sixteenth birthdays.

The other issue was the blatant nature of walking up to the bar and ordering a beer when everyone in the room knew we were underage, including the teachers and bar staff. Surely this would not be permitted and we would face the humiliation of a very public rejection in front of, you know, girls and everything.

When we got there and walked in, our fears were eased somewhat by the fact that everybody else already had an alcoholic drink in front of them and at least two of the teachers were taking their chaperoning duties very seriously by being quite drunk already. We both went for the compromise of ordering a half pint: lager for him and (I have to admit) cider for me. In my defence, I don't think I had ever even tasted beer at that point, being far too small to get served in the dodgier pubs in my hometown at the age of 14, like some of my peers. I wasn't even sure if I would like cider or if I could finish the whole glass.

A couple of hours later I was seven glasses in, only mildly intoxicated, and even had the confidence to buy a drink for a girl in the Upper Sixth, though not enough to actually ask her out or try and kiss her. Baby steps here.

I floated home, having discovered the joy of alcohol-induced self-confidence without making a complete fool of myself in the process.

I soon graduated on to pints and that year was filled with birthday drinks gatherings in the pub nearest to our school, where we all knew the rules of eighties apprentice drinking. Dress smartly, order politely, drink quietly, preferably in a corner away from the bar, where you are unlikely to disturb other drinkers if you do get a bit boisterous after a few drinks.

These rules still apply today. Most grown-ups are reasonably tolerant of slightly underage drinkers, because they can look back fondly on their own youth and remember doing it themselves, but, like the old adage about children, apprentice drinkers in pubs should always be seen and not heard.

By Upper Sixth I'd gone on to actual beer, and I've been a bitter drinker ever since. I can now confidently blame my teachers and the school for any or all of the failures in my life for setting me so early onto the road to depravity. It really is all their fault. Anyone know a good lawyer?

ROUND ETIQUETTE

On arrival at the pub, it is expected to enter into a certain amount of good-natured quarrelling over who will pay for the first round. This is done for reasons of friendship and camaraderie, and everyone concerned must make at least a reasonably concerted effort to buy the first round. They will then be thanked for their generosity.

Leaving the pub following the consumption of that first round, if you didn't pay for it, without buying a round yourself, is a sin so heinous it offends all right-thinking folk and may lead to a state of social exclusion lasting years.

Most people know this and it is a simple matter of self-policing. If three, four or five are in a round, each of them will take a turn to buy that round before it goes back to the first once again.

At this point it is acceptable for those with early starts, work in the morning, weak constitutions or tropical diseases in their system to break from the pack and go home. Those left can openly discuss whether the round system should continue or if a kitty would be better employed and, if so, just how much that should be. Someone , trusted by the others to be exceptionally honest with the cash collected (on pain of death or pariah status), will keep the kitty and become Kitty Meister. Their job is to order and pay for the drinks from then on. They are allowed to relinquish these duties to someone else if the pub is busy and the job of constantly queuing and ordering drinks is therefore too onerous to do for the rest of the evening.

There will of course be occasions in the life of a Professor of Pintfulness when they find themselves slightly out of kilter in the round system, having bought both the first and last rounds, leaving themselves more out of pocket than the rest of their drinking buddies. This slight financial misfortune should be taken on the chin and chalked up to drunken experience, and certainly never spoken of for fear of being considered both tight and churlish.

The above rules are so simple and so ingrained in beer-drinking pub culture that I really shouldn't have to put them in print but, if you have read them and think you may have been violating them in any way, you should take immediate action. Not only should you change your behaviour immediately, but you had better invest some serious cash in the future into overcompensating for your meanness, because – believe me when I say this – you already have a terrible reputation amongst your peer group. You just didn't know, because you didn't understand the rules.

URINAL ETIQUETTE*

I'm astonished I even have to spell this out to people, but I still come across quite flagrant breaches of urinal etiquette, even now.

If there are three urinals and none are being used, don't go to the middle one. This means that someone who joins you shortly afterwards has to awkwardly shuffle to your left or right. The proper position is quite obviously to take either the left or right of the three unused urinals, therefore enabling the next entrant to the gents to take the urinal furthest from you on the other side. Should neither of you have finished before a third person enters, he will at least be able to use his own judgement, based largely on the amount of space between urinals, before deciding whether to join this ad hoc gathering or take the easy route, by pretending to go for a dump and choosing a cubicle instead (remembering, of course, to avoid making too much noise and exposing his furtive urination in the process).

SPEAKING

On no account should you speak to another man while pissing. This is a cardinal sin and the height of bad manners. He is obviously at his most vulnerable and simply wishes to concentrate on syphoning the python in as swift and efficient a manner as possible, before leaving and continuing to drink alone or with friends.

* obviously this does not apply to all of our readers

You, on the other hand, are a stranger. A stranger with his cock in his hand. If this were a public park and you spoke to me like that, I could probably get away with bludgeoning you to death as an act of self-defence, and no jury would convict me. For some reason, however, you think that us both holding our manhoods at the same time is the right moment to comment on the weather, the pub and its beer, or the football match we have just been watching. It isn't.

Would you come up to me in the street and discuss such things with a stranger? No, of course not, so just because I am momentarily a captive audience does not give you the right to break the silence.

FARTING

The one exception to the no-speaking rule concerns farting at the urinal near mine. In this case it is permitted to mumble an 'excuse me' by way of apology for inflicting your arse-gas upon me. This does not mean I want to hear you groan in exertion or pleasure and I *absolutely do not want* to hear you proudly say, 'Better out than in.'

WHISTLING

No one wants to hear you whistle. Ever. Got that?
    Good.
    It's distracting; annoying; sounds terrible, unless you are one of those unlikely people who can actually carry a tune in which case ... no, even then, just don't. What are you, some kind

of psycho? That's what people will think, as the flow of urine immediately runs dry and they tense against your tuneless dirge. The level of self-confidence required to whistle amongst other men at a urinal means you are either massively thick-skinned, hugely egotistical and/or dangerously deranged. We don't want to be peeing next to anyone like that.

SINGING

See above.

If anything, this is worse than whistling, as you come across as even more crazed. You might think you are singing a song because you are full of the joys of spring, yet you seem to have forgotten that your hand is full of something else and so is mine. We both need silence right now so we can finish what we are doing and get the hell out of here.

TYPES OF PINT

There are many brands of beer and a lot of people are aware of most of them, but few are familiar with the different types of pint. It takes a Professor of Pintfulness to distinguish between these. See how many of them you recognise:

THE QUICK PINT

In some cases, this might actually refer to a single, solitary and swift beer that is quaffed in around a quarter of an hour, perhaps while waiting for a train to arrive. More often, however, it is a well-intentioned but naïve suggestion from a friend or colleague that implies you both have the self-discipline to stop at one pint once you have entered a pub. This ridiculous notion is instantly defeated by round etiquette (see 'Rules of the Pub'), which denotes that one of you has to buy both pints, as it is incredibly bad form for you to purchase your beer while your colleague buys their own when you have arrived together. You don't want the barman to think you have been badly brought up or have never previously darkened the doors of a pub.

As soon as you or your mate have bought the first round, it goes without saying that there will be a second pint (at the very least), which will be paid for by whoever didn't buy the first one. By this point a two-pint-mellow will have descended upon you both and one of you is likely to suggest a 'quick one for the road' but that idea will also flounder on the rocks of round etiquette, because only one of you can pay for it and the other will have to wait their turn. Your 'quick pint' will have swiftly become a four-pinter. The downing of the fourth pint is likely to lead to a 'fuck-it pint'.

THE FUCK-IT PINT

This is the pint that signals the abandonment of whatever restraint you had previously talked about on entering the pub or just before doing so. Your well-intentioned idea of just having a quick pint or two will be forgotten as soon as you take a sip of the fuck-it pint, and a beer drinking session – which will involve writing off the entire evening – will now ensue.

THE CRAFTY PINT

This is a pint that is quickly taken while between obligations, such as work or chores that cannot be fully side-stepped or entirely put off. If you leave a client meeting early and go for a pint before heading back to the office, then this qualifies as a crafty pint. If you stop off on the way back from a DIY store – having picked up tiles, grouting, sealant and fiddly tools for the application of said materials – you can easily steal twenty minutes, with the explanation that the first store 'didn't have a grout float' and you were forced to go elsewhere for it. By their very definition, crafty pints involve a certain amount of guile and opportunism, so they tend to taste approximately twice as good as normal pints.

THE SNEAKY PINT

I've got a mate – let's call him Steve (because that's his actual name) – who derives great joy from what he calls a sneaky pint. This is a beer that can only be enjoyed if duplicity is used, which only adds to its appeal. It's forbidden fruit or forbidden hops at least.

His illicit pint comes on a Friday evening when he returns home from work to announce that it has been a long week, everyone is tired, especially his poor wife, wouldn't it be great if no one had to cook that night and what a great idea it would be to pick up a takeaway instead. Being the hunter-gatherer that he is, he will take it upon himself to go manfully into the night to bring back the twenty-first-century equivalent of a woolly mammoth, or whatever Neolithic man slaughtered when he was peckish (look it up if you care that much, do I have to do everything?).

Once he has secured the necessary pass-out from his wife, along with her gratitude because she doesn't have to prepare a meal, Steve sets out, with a spring in his step and a twinkle in his eye, to the nearest Chinese takeaway, coincidentally situated yards from one of the best pubs in town. He orders food for the whole family, carefully adding a portion of those mushroom and pak choi things, covered in a sauce that looks a bit like snot. For some inexplicable reason his wife loves these, so he can win extra Brownie points: 'I got these especially for you, pet.'

Once his order is placed, the woman behind the counter always says the same thing, 'Fifteen minutes?'

He always gives the same reply: 'Could you make it twenty?'

He then goes off to the pub for a 'sneaky pint', enjoying every illicit sip all the more, because his wife thinks he is sitting in the waiting room of the takeaway.

Now I'm pretty sure that if he actually said, 'Do you fancy a takeaway and do you mind if I have a quick pint while I'm waiting for it?' she would probably say 'No problem' – but that, of course, would ruin the fun for him entirely, as well as defeating the object of his sneaky pint.

THE WELL-EARNED PINT

DIY

Nothing tastes better than a well-earned pint. When you've been toiling at some form of Ikea-created, DIY torture for hours, when the words 'easily-assembled' and 'snap-fit' come back to haunt you as you try again and again to get the 'bastard-thing' to 'cocking-well-stay-together', your morale plummets. Days like these are usually hot and sunny for some reason, and this will leave you feeling like you are severely missing out. Your kids are outside playing, your single mates are down the pub, your other half might already be questioning whether you have the brains and ability to put together a simple bookcase, and right now you are feeling like a complete failure. She may even secretly be wondering to herself whether her life would have been better if she had married that other bloke who asked her out years ago. She's possibly stalking him on Facebook even now to see if he's still single, and who could blame her? I mean, what kind of a man *are* you if you can't even –

Stop.

It really is hammer time.

Lesser men than you would take that hammer and smash what was left of Billy's fucking bookcase into tiny pieces, but not you. You won't be defeated by this giant Swedish jigsaw puzzle.

Why? Because you're a man and you come from a long line of men (and women obviously, everyone does). You can recall your father asking you to pass him a wrench while he peered under the bonnet of that ancient, second-hand car he drove back in the seventies; the one that ground to a halt halfway through every holiday. Your father would scoff at the notion of taking it to an actual garage, then he'd rebuild half the engine till it worked perfectly again.

You can picture him now, looking down from his cloud scornfully (for some reason his hands and arms are still covered in the oil from that day long ago), and he is shaking his head. Don't you remember your grandad fitting an entire kitchen on his own or how he rewired his old house to avoid troubling an electrician? While you, my own son, sometimes struggle to insert a bulb into that fancy new light fighting that hangs in your living room.

That's it, you decide. I shall *not* be defeated by a mere bookcase. And so you have another go, then another, and you keep going until finally you have done it!

The bookcase is complete. It has shelves and everything and, apart from one little blemish on the side where you were a tiny bit too enthusiastic with the hammer (and no one will notice that, right?), it looks good!

Now you feel like Harrison Ford in *Witness* when he helps his new Amish friends build a barn. You don't have Kelly McGillis to deliver a refreshing glass of lemonade, but you have something better! You're off to the pub.

No one objects. They know the sweat, blood, tears and toil that went into that 'fucking bookcase', as it will hereafter be known in your family's folklore, especially by your 4-year old, who overheard this and will gleefully repeat it a week from now on a play date, in front of your wife, three other kids and their mortified mums.

Today, though, you will walk into that pub like a giant, for you have made something with your own hands. It's important to choose the right pub for this moment. One with white vans and pickup trucks parked outside is the right option. You might wear a tie to work and sit in front of a computer all day pumping market research stats into spreadsheets no one will ever read, but today you are a blue-collar man. If only the pub had swing doors like in those old westerns; then you could really make an entrance.

You'll have that aura about you now: one caused by physical toil. You might even still be a bit sweaty; it's warm out after all and that first-floor bedroom can be a bit muggy in the daytime. Order your pint and drink this one at the bar. Let every plumber and builder in the place see you and maybe even nod in recognition.

I guarantee that pint will be one of the most delicious you have ever tasted, because nothing quite matches a pint earned.

5-A-Side Football

The call comes out of the blue. You've not played football for years, and barely at all since leaving school, but they are a man short, desperate and the game is tomorrow. You're chuffed to be even asked, it's as if they assume you must be good at the game and not because you are literally the last male in the office.

You rashly agree and even go and buy an overpriced pair of those trainers with the special knobbly bits on the bottom that almost guarantees a broken ankle if you stop suddenly on AstroTurf, and may or not be called 'blades'; you have no idea. It feels weird even walking in them, and you can't justify the amount you paid, even if you are determined to start playing every week from now on, because you're over 30 and that belly won't get rid of itself. You stuff them in an old sports bag you had to wipe the dust from and don't tell your other half how much you shelled out for them. She's got more expensive shoes anyway, you're sure of it. Those ones she bought for her sister's wedding for example, and you doubt she'll ever even wear them again. No, this is a value purchase and an investment, in the future and yourself.

You go to bed that night dreaming of scoring goals the way you used to on the playground or for the school team ... okay, the school team's reserves. You can still recall every goal you've ever scored, which is strange because you can't remember a single thing you did at work last week that filled you with any sense of pride or pleasure. Never mind, the game is tomorrow evening, it's a grudge match against another department and you can't wait. You've got this.

Your enthusiasm is slightly dampened when you meet the other team. They play every week, in an actual league. Their kit matches, whereas you are wearing a fifteen-year-old Premier League top that dates both you and it. It bulges around that belly of yours in an uncomfortable manner, but that's okay because you have been given a torn, slightly stained, yellow bib to put over it.

The first half is a nightmare. Is it really six–nil to them already? It should be more. Your first attempt to kick the ball was an air shot and your second a pass that went straight to the toes of an opposing player who slammed it past your goalkeeper. You almost cause a mass brawl when your mistimed tackle on the same player is so late it could have occurred next Wednesday. His teammates and yours are all wondering if you actually meant to decapitate him and you get a bit of cautious respect from everyone after that.

Let's be honest, you are shot now, completely gone. It's only surely a matter of whether your heart or your legs give out first. Half time can't come soon enough. Everything hurts, aches or refuses to cooperate. This is awful, just awful. Why did you agree to do it, you fool? You're simply not the man you used to be.

Then something strange happens. The second half kicks off and you are not entirely terrible. You actually trap the ball and it doesn't career over the boards. Buoyed by this, you make a tackle and a couple of passes. The opposition, still six-nil up, understandably run out of steam, and the rag-tag collection of part-timers on your side actually put up a fight. Your goalie makes a couple of saves and you've got that one bloke who is quite good in a way you would never be if you trained and played every day for the rest of your life. That skinny bloke in your department who looked like a lazy goalhanger actually steers the ball into the net and it's game on!

The match finishes 9–4 but you don't mind; you expected it to be 14–nil. There is a certain amount of glory in avoiding that outcome. You have run your heart out, your face is red, your shirt and bib are stained with sweat. Everyone agrees you did okay and 'got stuck in', which is sufficient praise on a football field for someone who hasn't played the game in sixteen years. You even almost scored with that one shot from a distance, and so you'll relive that moment time and time again while pretending to concentrate on your spreadsheets.

The best bit is afterwards in the pub, when all of the key moments are relived, including your terrible foul, and you gain the nickname 'Vinnie' after Vinnie Jones, a man you would normally despise – but not today. The accompanying pint has only ever tasted this good when you wrestled with that Billy bookcase. Somehow this is even better, because you are with your mates (they are officially mates now, not just colleagues). You are a team. A band of brothers.

It's a pint earned, through athletic endeavour, so that makes you an athlete! In the morning you won't be able to walk, but for sure you'll be back again next week.

PLAYING AWAY FROM HOME

Football and Pintfulness go hand in hand. There is a direct correlation between the number of pints you need and the size of the humiliation you have just witnessed, as your own personal 'greatest team in the land' are thrashed by a sheikh-sponsored side full of former Real Madrid players. Your best player cost under £10 million, earns sixty grand a week, and *still* can't take a corner without hitting the first man, a skill most pub-side players have mastered even with a colossal hangover.

Of course, some away fixtures require several pints just to give you the confidence to walk to a hostile ground. Leeds United and West Ham spring to mind, but Millwall away should never be attempted without at least five pints inside you and a thick coat (preferably made of chain mail) to cover every inch of your own team's colours.

Add in an extra pint – for cruel cup semi-final losses, tragic penalty shoot-out defeats or crushing home losses in a local derby – then drink them while wondering what your life would have been like, if you'd been born one of those lucky people who can simply say 'I don't like football.'

Personally, I am a long-suffering Newcastle United fan, and if there is anyone who deserves a pint more than us I have yet to come across them.

SEDIMENTARY, MY DEAR WATSON: FUSSY DRINKERS

We all have that one friend who raises the glass and examines their pint suspiciously before drinking it, like a detective looking for clues at the scene of a particularly puzzling murder scene, and they do it *every single time*. Everyone has had a cloudy pint and it's perfectly acceptable to return it. After all, the cost of a beer these days is roughly akin to the amount your grandparents put down as a deposit to secure the purchase of their first house.

Who hasn't been poured a beer that looks like water from the Thames Estuary? It's usually a sign you're the first person to ask for that particular beer in weeks and it has been sitting in the pipes patiently waiting for you all that time, gathering algae.

I was once even served a pint of line cleaner by a particularly unobservant teenage barman. I had ordered this for my father-in-law, who had just been told by doctors that he was allowed to drink again, following a reasonably long hiatus for heart treatment. The young barman actually poured an entire pint of the yellowish, bleachy substance that someone had forgotten to drain from the lines before reconnecting beer to the pump. My FIL, whose eyesight isn't great without his glasses, was about to reach for it to take a sip, but I spotted it just in time and told the uncomprehending lad just what he had poured. Had I allowed my FIL to take that sip we would have been straight back to the hospital, and the pub would have had a lot of explaining to do.

That was an extreme case (and a thankfully rare one) but your mate takes their scrutiny of a pint to the extreme. They're about to show it to the barman because they're convinced it looks a bit dodgy, but first they need you to agree with them. 'Look at that,' they'll demand, frowning at their hundredth pint this year. Don't fall for it. We all get a duff pint now and then, but not every single time like this nitpicker. Tell them that they're imagining things or simply offer them a knife and fork to eat it with.

DON'T BE THAT GUY:
WEDDINGS AND DRINKING

Why do so many people get drunk at weddings? It's because they are rank amateurs in the art of Pintfulness and haven't learned the crucial need to pace yourself during an all-day event that largely centres on alcohol.

Meeting for a pint next to the church before the ceremony; heading straight back into it once it's over, while the bride and groom are being expensively photographed amid the gravestones; then hitting a reception that involves mixing champagne with wine and even more beer – it's the kind of passport to disaster that the organisers of Brexit would be proud of.

Far better to remember that a wedding is an Olympic-sized-swimming-pool of an event, where sipping not supping should be encouraged. It's an occasion for professional practitioners of Pintfulness, not mere amateurs.

Leering at bridesmaids, pawing other people's girlfriends, throwing up in public, heckling the speeches: all of these will guarantee you infamy that will last not just years but decades. Everyone remembers their wedding day, so they will all remember you. Every time those photos come out to be shown to the kids and grandkids, your name will crop up, so a whole new generation can humiliate you anew and your ears will rightfully burn.

The moto for wedding drinking is clear and simple: non-skaters off the ice! Unless, of course, you *want* to loom long and large in anecdotes told by the happy couple, who will regale everyone with tales of 'that guy' who very nearly almost ruined their big day, at least until they are finally divorced.

WHAT DID I DO?
THE CHRISTMAS BASH

You've been working hard all year and the day to let your hair down is finally here. It's the office Christmas party! Go crazy, right?

Wrong. On no account go crazy! No Professor of Pintfulness ever went crazy at a Christmas party.

Keep asking yourself this question at regular intervals, throughout the day and evening: 'Would I be doing this in front of my boss, office-wife and co-workers if I wasn't absolutely shitfaced?' If the answer is 'no' then stop *immediately*. Better still, don't begin any of that behaviour at all. This covers dancing, snogging, snog-dancing, dance-snogging or any other form of activity that involves shuffling feet, flailing limbs or lips being inappropriately welded together.

If you absolutely *must* have an affair at work, this is the one day when you simply have to keep it well under wraps.

I started my working life (the one before I decided to just make stuff up for a living) at the beginning of the nineties; a decade of lad and ladette culture that was the high and also low point of incautious, drink-fuelled, festive misbehaviour. As a young man, I witnessed all kinds of shenanigans, though I am obviously duty-bound to avoid mentioning names and details, even now.

Suffice to say, senior management, who used to urge you not to 'poke the payroll', would exhibit staggering hypocrisy for one day a year by getting drunk and trying (and usually failing) to 'charm' young female employees into their beds, locked offices or stationery cupboards. I've seen people get drunk and sing sectarian songs while those on the other side of the religious divide sat in the same room and quietly fumed. Fights have broken out, or come close to it, and people have been banned from host venues for shagging in the public toilets. And that was on one of the quieter years.

You will probably not experience that level of temptation these days, because the company-funded office party is more or less over and who can afford to get that drunk on their own coin? Thirty years ago, employees would gripe if the venue or free food was not up to the usual standard. Before the last company office Christmas party I attended, half a dozen years ago, I was informed I would have to pay for my own booze, meal and train fare into London, running up a sizeable bill in the process. I wouldn't have minded if I could have just said 'no thanks', but it was strongly hinted to me that the meal was unofficially compulsory, lest I look like I wasn't a team player. This was not my idea of a 'Merry Christmas'.

Combine a lack of company largesse and HR being all over this kind of occasion these days like a bunch of former KGB agents, and you won't even be able to make jokes about having 'pulled a cracker' without being hauled up on a disciplinary. It's probably for the best – but why, then, do I miss the inappropriate drunken shenanigans of yesteryear?

Probably because my office party is a lonely affair these days. As a writer, I'm the only one in attendance and the landlord of my local pub definitely frowns on drunken, public displays of affection when there is no one else in the room with you.

WAKE ME UP BEFORE YOU GO-GO

This is not a reference to a casual, possibly Tinder-inspired, one-night stand. This is a page about that all-important last train home

It used to cost fourteen quid to get to Harpenden from Luton Airport by cab back in the day. How do I know this? Because I used to live there, and even the finest and most experienced practitioners of Pintfulness occasionally canes it so hard in their youth that, as soon as the train starts rocking on the tracks, the welcoming oblivion of sleep beckons them.

Virtually everyone has climbed off a train and noticed the person opposite is in an absolute coma, leaving them with a moral dilemma: to wake or not to wake? If this is their stop, they will thank you profusely, but if they are heading to a station at the end of the line, they will be less than happy and violence might ensue, causing you to miss your own stop.

A sticker with the words 'Wake me up at [NAME OF STATION]' placed on the chest will leave fellow passengers in no doubt.

This will help you avoid the fate of an old drinking buddy of mine who used to get the Great Western train home to Reading from Paddington, and once accidentally woke up, following a medium-to-heavy, Christmas-inspired drinking session, to find himself not just in Cardiff but in Cardiff sidings. He was stranded on an empty, cold train for the entire night, with no idea what service it would form in the morning, giving him a very long time to regret the folly of that 'one last pint'.

YOU MARK MY WORDS:
THE PUB BORE

Not to be confused with the beer bore (who bores everyone with only one subject: beer), the pub bore will spout off on a wide range of subjects on which he believes himself to be an expert. Usually found in his natural habitat (perched on a stool at the end of the bar), he'll be nursing a pint, desperately trying to hold court with anyone stupid enough to listen to him. This man has a large number of firmly held opinions, nearly all of which have been arrived at without the assistance of facts or common sense.

His body language is a dead giveaway: shoulders and head turned slightly inwards, so he doesn't miss anyone approaching the bar. If he knows you at all, beware. This is the point at which you are most vulnerable. Until you have ordered, been served and paid for that drink, you are cornered, trapped like a rat. Preferably speak only when spoken to; a gruff and preoccupied-sounding response along the lines of 'Now then, Brian' will suffice (it's amazing how statistically likely it is that a pub bore will be called Brian).

On no account should you ask a pub bore how he is. This will elicit a lengthy response about his health; marriage, if he still has one (unlikely); job, if he still has one (highly unlikely); or the state of the country and its political situation. You will then be forced to stand there uncomfortably while he regales you with opinions on what is wrong and how it could all be easily fixed if only we were brave enough to:

a) Kick out the Prime Minister
b) Kick out the party of the Prime Minister
c) Nationalise everything
d) Privatise everything
e) Be more like America
f) Be less like America
g) Quit the EU
h) Rejoin the EU

All this is dependent on his political leanings.

All pub bores think they know it all, but it's not just politics they pronounce on. The pub bore will offer life advice too. Don't take it. Do the opposite in fact; if he had a life, the pub bore wouldn't be sitting in the pub every day. He'd be at home with a wife and kids. This won't stop him telling you exactly how to live your life.

The strategies he recommends should be treated with the suspicion usually reserved for large investments in time-share, holiday-homes in Iran.

My favourite pub bore experience dates back thirty years to my time as a barman. We had a diminutive regular called Brian (told you) who worked at the local bookies and came in every day to order his usual beer in his tried-and-trusted way. 'Pint of Scotch, kid!' he'd call. One day he must have had more than normal, because this tiny, ageing, really quite *grubby* man, with greasy hair and yellow, nicotine-stained fingers, started to regale us all with stories of his youthful prowess with women. I'll reproduce his exact words here for you now:

'Any man that cannot satisfy five women in a single night is a disgrace to manhood!' He proclaimed, then added for good measure, 'They used to call me *the Machine*.'

Then he carried on as if nothing unusual had occurred, while we tried to pick ourselves up off the floor.

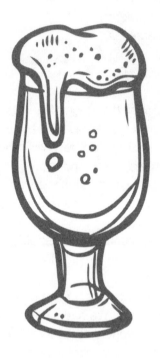

I FOUGHT THE LAW AND I WON:
THE LOCK IN

You cannot truly describe yourself as a Professor of Pintfulness until you have been included in one of its more sacred rituals: The Lock-In.

More flexible licensing laws, involving extended hours beyond the traditional 11.00pm curfew, might have slightly diminished the appeal of a landlord-sanctioned lock-in. But *true* scholars of Pintfulness know that there is nothing quite like being in a pub when it is closed to lesser mortals.

Picture the scene: you are a regular in a cosy, unspoilt, non-chain hostelry and the night is drawing to a close. Non-regulars are thinning out. The majority drift away without being asked; some may want to linger but are given nonverbal hints – finished glasses are immediately swept away, the table nearest to them sprayed with that anti-bac stuff and wiped down with a cloth, chairs straightened and hard stares of disapproval sent their way – until they feel uncomfortable enough to depart.

Then, with a touching solemnity, the landlord draws the curtains across the windows and locks the front door.

In films, the locking-in of drinkers in a bar usually signals the commencement of a massive brawl or gangster-style punishment beating. Not in this case. The landlord will then mumble something along the lines of 'Anymore for anymore?' and in an orderly and dignified manner, they will replenish everyone's drinks.

Congratulations, you are now breaking the law and so are they – or, at the very least, the terms of their licensing agreement. Your beer tastes even better because it has the added ingredient of illegality. You can imagine yourself a member of a small gang of devil-may-care bandidos, rebels without a cause who are flouting the normal rules of society. It's not quite anarchy but it tastes like it and the taste is good.

Pat yourself on the back, because you have been evaluated by your fellow drinkers and the landlord. You have been examined and passed the test. You are officially 'alright'.

In the context of the British pub there are few higher accolades.

NO MEETINGS: CAMRA

In that classic nineties black comedy *Grosse Pointe Blank*, John Cusack's character is asked by Dan Ayckroyd's fellow hitman to join a union or face assassination. His response? 'This union. Is there going to be meetings?'

When he is assured there will be, he demurs, 'No meetings.' He hates meetings.

Who doesn't? Anyone who has ever had to sit through one, which is most of us, must surely agree that meetings absolutely suck.

Why then, when given the opportunity to escape the mundanity of office life for a relaxing session devoted to Pintfulness, would you possibly turn this into a meeting, with actual minutes and decisions to be made on whether there is a need to have a policy on this, that or the other?

This is why no true Professor of Pintfulness will ever find themselves chairing a meeting of CAMRA. In many ways, the Campaign for Real Ale is a fine body, which should be commended for caring so much about drinking and pubs, the livelihood of landlords and the quality of the beers on offer to Pintfulness practitioners. All of this is worthy stuff, but therein lies the problem. You can't be worthy *and* be 'in the pint'. There are no minutes taken during Pintfulness.

Applaud the work of CAMRA from a distance, while refraining from actually attending one of its meetings.

SNAKE'S VENOM:
THE WORLD'S STRONGEST BEER

The aptly named 'Snake's Venom' is the world's strongest beer. It has an original gravity ten times that of even a strong beer. Most beers have an OG of between 3.5 per cent and 5 per cent. Snake's Venom has a mind-altering *67.5 per cent.*

Considering that the usual OG of spirits like whiskey and brandy rarely exceeds 40 per cent, it is astonishing that anyone might even attempt to make a beer with such a high alcoholic content. This is a beer to be sipped or, unless you're a complete masochist, actively avoided.

This witch's brew was created by the Scottish Brewmeister brewery and they apparently advise everyone to only drink one bottle per session. Well, that's alright then. I'm so glad they are responsible.

THE TEMPLE OF BEER

There is a temple in Thailand that is very special indeed. It stands out, even in a country with more than 40,000 Buddhist temples, because it is made entirely from bottles of beer. Construction on *Wat Pa Maha Chedi Kaew*, which literally translates as the 'Wilderness Temple of the Great Glass Pagoda', began in 1984 and was completed in around two years.

Built in the Khun Han district of Sisaket province, the monks there wanted to use green and sustainable materials while still helping to encourage waste disposal. They used 1.5 million empty Heineken and Chang beer bottles to complete the temple, but they didn't stop there. The monks added prayer rooms, a crematorium, a water tower and even visitor toilets, as well as housing for the monks; all made from beer bottles. There are now more than twenty buildings surrounding the temple, and in case you are wondering what they do with all of the bottle tops, they use them to make decorative mosaics.

The monks have implied all of the empty beer bottles are donated or they find them just discarded in the street – but what if they run out and need to add on an extension? Do they rush out and buy a few cases, drink them in a hurry, then start building again in the morning, once the hangovers have subsided? I like to think so.

GHOSTING FROM THE ROOM

Every Professor of Pintfulness needs to know the exact moment to leave a party/room/pub but that's only half the battle. No one ever just leaves. *They* won't let you. Professors of Pintfulness understand this: you have to *ghost*.

The moment when you realise you can no longer drink any more, unless you want to lose the power of your speech/legs/reason/all three, you need to be ready to ghost. This point is often reached away from the hubbub of the bar, amid the calm backdrop of the pub toilet, sometimes while staring into the mirror while gripping the sides of the wash basin to avoid falling over.

Amateurs usually make a fundamental mistake at this point. They go back into the bar, actually speak to the group of mates they have been drinking with, confess they can consume no more and want to go home. In the tried-and-trusted manner of true friends, they will forbid this. There will be much talk of staying to have 'just one more' and to 'not be so boring'. This kind of mild joshing should not work on adults but, when said adults are very drunk, it is remarkably effective. Several drinks later, the person who should have left an hour ago is now swaying down the street and falling into bushes. All because they didn't know how to 'ghost'.

There is an art to ghosting. You head for the toilet, empty that bursting bladder (to avoid any potentially embarrassing, public-urination incidents/arrests on the way home), splash some water on your face (if that's what it takes to concentrate the mind), then leave the room and march purposefully from the building by whichever exit is furthest from your fellow drinkers, before they notice you are gone. Then go directly home.

You will take a bit of stick in the morning, but this will be via Messenger and not face to face. You will also be sober and less susceptible to ego-stinging accusations of being boring, so you can simply message back that you had a great time but had to go because you were hammered. Job done.

I once went to the toilet in a bar and decided I had an urgent need to ghost. When I walked back into the room, the mate I'd been drinking with for hours was fast asleep in a chair. A true friend would have woken him up to make sure he was alright and could get home okay. I was not a true friend that night. I was drunk, so I ghosted and even bought a Chinese takeaway on the walk home.

Why didn't I wake him? Because I knew he would never let me leave. He was so drunk that night that he doesn't remember me ghosting from the bar or being left there all on his tod. I assume he simply woke up, confused, then drifted silently home ... like a ghost.

COME AND HAVE A GO IF YOU THINK YOU ARE DRUNK ENOUGH: FIGHTING DRUNK

Alcohol can be a depressant, and for some people, beer can bring out their worst side. We've all heard the term 'fighting drunks', but there can be few ideas worse than picking a fight when you are pissed. Reflections and reactions are impaired by alcohol, which is just what you need when you are swinging punches and dodging them from the other guy. Inhibitions and fear are also lessened – but fear has a purpose. It can keep us from harm or indulging in high-risk activities, like starting a fight with someone who is likely to knock what remaining sense we have out of us.

You can hurt them too. I realise you are probably thinking that's the *point* of a fight, to hurt the other guy before they can hurt you, but you only have to pick up a newspaper to see why punching someone hard, without considering the consequences, is a very bad idea indeed.

Earlier this year a former soldier was jailed for six years for manslaughter when he punched a man outside a nightclub who subsequently died. It wasn't the actual punch that killed him. It rarely is. The fall afterwards – when the victim, who was a father of two, hit his head on the pavement – proved fatal. He was unconscious as he fell, so neither he nor the man who hit him could control what happened next.

In Scotland, during the last calendar year, six people died in separate incidents as a result of a single punch, causing untold grief to the victim's families and a lifetime of regret for the fighting drunk who accidentally killed him.

I have said it elsewhere but in this case I really mean it. Don't be that guy.

EATING'S NOT CHEATING:
LINING THE STOMACH

A Professor of Pintfulness knows the need to protect the inside of the stomach before a night out by covering it with a layer of food. Those who think 'eating is cheating' before a night 'on the pop' will find out to their cost that they are far more hammered than their mates, who sensibly stuff down a burger and chips before hitting the pub. Science proves that lining the stomach is not only desirable but a must, because food soaking up the booze prevents alcohol from quickly hitting the bloodstream and gives your liver more time to break it all down.

The neurotransmitters in your brain are particularly susceptible to the effects of alcohol in the bloodstream, which isn't good as it's their job to send messages from the brain to the rest of the body. This is why very drunk people suddenly lose control of their limbs and why drunks fall over. Decision-making can be impaired and your judgement can fly out of the window, causing romantic entanglements that seem like a good idea at the time but less so in the cold light of day. It can also affect your inhibitions, which is why really drunk people have been known to remove their clothes, dance on tables and snog people they would normally ignore.

So, if you don't want to end up dancing naked in the pub, have a pizza before you have those beers.

THE EYE OF THE BEER HOLDER:
BEER GOGGLES

It is a scientifically proven fact that consumption of alcohol can make someone appear more attractive, but it is rarely the person doing the actual drinking who improves in appearance. No, it is the one seen through the eye of the drunken beholder who benefits from the soft-filtering effects of beer.

If you view a moderately attractive person through the prism of beer, they may begin to resemble a Hollywood star, and before you know it, your drunken self is focusing on them with a vigour that could lead to a regrettable liaison.

In order to see if there was any actual science behind the concept of beer goggles, researchers brought eighty students into a bar in 2003, then got them to rate the attractiveness of subjects from the opposite sex in photographs. Some drank and some didn't. The results were published in the scientific journal *Addiction*.

Their conclusion was that the students who drank alcohol were more generous with their markings. All the students were straight, and the researchers found this phenomenon occurred among both men and women, as long as they were rating the opposite sex (when they were asked to rate members of their *own* sex, the drinkers were no more generous with their marks than the non-drinkers). This conclusively proves that nature's aphrodisiac is not asparagus or oysters but beer, and any other alcoholic beverage that can put rose-tinted glasses on you.

Furthermore, in 2013, French researchers found that, the more alcohol subjects consumed, the more attractive they found themselves, though there is one obvious and fairly big caveat here – they were French and the French often think they are gorgeous.

Whatever the science behind this, there is usually some common sense attached to it too. Alcohol is known to lower the inhibitions, which means you are more likely to actually make a move on someone if you have been drinking. Alcohol also causes endorphins and dopamine to be released into our brains. These are chemicals that make us more likely to seek a reward, such as a nice meal or a night of passion. When you combine this with the beer goggle effect, it's no wonder lots of people get it on after drinking and it's a good job they do, otherwise many of us probably wouldn't be here.

A WARM GLOW:
THE BEER BLANKET

This is a widely recognised phenomenon, particularly if you come from a cold part of the country. It starts with the notion that you don't need to wear a coat, because you are only going to the pub and won't be exposed to the cold for long. The return journey is, of course, covered. Who needs a jacket when they have a 'beer blanket'? This is not something handed out by benign landlords to keep you toasty on the way home, nor is it one of those covers you are given by restaurants in London because they have run out of tables and have to seat you outdoors in freezing conditions. No, it's not a physical thing at all, but a condition that experienced beer drinkers will recognise. On your way into the pub in the early evening you feel the cold, but you emerge hours later, when the temperature is significantly lower, and don't feel it at all.

This must mean that beer warms us from the inside, raises our internal body temperature and keeps us snug all the way home, right?

Wrong.

We might not feel the cold but it's still there and affecting our body in exactly the same way – we just don't notice. It's the same for other physical sensations, which are also deadened by alcohol intake. If someone punches you when you are sober, it hurts; if they hit you when you have had a few then it probably won't sting as much until you are sober again; if you thump an alcoholic they might not feel it till next Tuesday.

This is also the reason why some men – ahem – but never Professors of Pintfulness, and certainly not me, you understand – occasionally fail to rise to the occasion when … anyway enough of that.

Beer blankets! We were talking about beer blankets, damn it.

A beer blanket is very useful to keep the chill from you on short-to-medium-sized walks home after a night in the pub, but should not be relied upon if you have to trudge for miles, and must *never* be trusted if your walk back from a bar to your hotel room is somewhere less balmy than the UK, like Helsinki or Moscow.

Every year, someone passes out outdoors from excessive drinking and sometimes these poor unfortunates never wake up. Back in 2016, a 21-year-old woman left a party in Wisconsin, USA, following an argument. Dressed only in shorts and a tank top, she was so drunk she did not realise the temperature had plummeted to -27 degrees by then, and she tragically died of hypothermia on her walk home.

A BOTTLE OF DOG:
NEWCASTLE BROWN ALE

Newcastle Brown Ale is indeed a Brown Ale that was brewed in Newcastle (there is a clue in the name). Served in a clear glass bottle, with a distinctive taste and original gravity of 4.7 per cent, the beer was an instant hit and its appeal grew, both in and out of the region where it was born.

Production of the beer began in 1927 at the Tyne Brewery. The famous five-pointed blue star was added to the bottle a year later, and a little over half a century afterwards, it adorned the black and white shirts of Newcastle United when the brewery became the club's main sponsor. By the 1990s, Newcastle Brown was the most widely distributed alcoholic product in the UK.

The beer has become so popular it is sold to forty countries and around half of its production is exported to the United States, the land of watery-tasting beer. Maybe that's why proper beer drinkers over there appreciate the good stuff. Clint Eastwood, a proper beer drinker if ever there was one, has publicly described Newcastle Brown Ale as his favourite beer. If it's good enough for Dirty Harry?

If you drink this in Newcastle then you might want to refer to it as 'Newcy Broon' or, if you really want to fit in, 'a bottle of dog'. This strange canine reference is explained by the long-standing tradition of a man excusing himself because he has to 'go and see a man about a dog' instead of actually admitting he is off to the pub for a broon. Oh, and you should always pour the contents of the bottle into a half-pint glass before sipping it, not a pint.

Newcastle Brown Ale was last brewed in Newcastle in 2005, before moving up the road to Dunston, then further afield to the John Smith's brewery in Tadcaster. If that wasn't enough of a blow to its north-east regional identity, then worse was to follow. In a tragic development, the parent company, Heineken, decided that most of Newcastle Brown Ale's production would move out of the country to the Zoeterwoude Brewery in the Netherlands, so now I suppose it's really Zoeterwoude Brown Ale, but that doesn't have quite the same ring to it.

SEXIST BEER

Sexism is rightly frowned upon by most people these days. It still exists, of course, but more and more people are calling it out in the workplace, in schools and in higher education. Hopefully, each new generation of women will experience less of it.

Why, then, does the brewing trade still think it's okay to make and market beers like these?

Old Growler Growler Brewery
Piddle in the Hole Wyre Piddle Brewery
The Hairy Beaver Pine Ridge Brewery
Leg Spreader Route 2 Brews Brewery
Dizzy Blonde Robinsons Brewery
Slack Alice Abrahals Brewery

You may have noticed that the one thing these beers all have in common is a name so staggeringly sexist that it's a wonder they haven't been banned. Actually, they have been – but only just. It took until 2019 for it to finally happen, but the Great British Beer Festival will from now on exclude any beer with a sexist or misogynistic name. This proves that the brewing industry is somewhat lagging behind the rest of the world, but is belatedly choosing to get its house in order.

According to research by CAMRA, only 17 per cent of women drink beer regularly. That might be down to taste or tradition, but beer festivals selling ales with sexist or downright misogynistic names probably don't help to entice females into a world of Pintfulness.

The research also showed that 68 per cent of women said they would not buy beer if it was advertised in a sexist way. You would have thought that was so bleeding obvious you wouldn't need to commission research to tell you it in the twenty-first century.

A LICENCE TO DRINK

The sale and consumption of alcohol is regulated in the UK by licensing laws. They are not quite as old or as stringent as the German *Reinheitsgebot*, but you break them at your peril. Lose your local-authority-granted licence and you could be closed down.

The best known aspect of UK licensing law is the age limit. You have to be an adult to drink alcohol in pubs, so at least 18 years of age, aside from cases where the drinking is done with a meal, when it is permitted to have some alcohol at the age of 16 or 17.

When I was growing up (at a time when dinosaurs still roamed the earth) and approaching the age when drinking legally seemed a fair way away, the age restriction seemed little more than a guideline that landlords could choose to ignore if it suited them. We knew that at 16 (and looking about 14), we would probably still get served if we behaved ourselves. I was in my twenties before things tightened up and IDs were needed, creating a burgeoning market for false ones.

'TIME, GENTLEMEN, PLEASE!'

Until relatively recently, the hours during which pubs could serve alcohol were quite strictly regulated. They could open at 11.00 a.m. but had to call time and shut at 11.00 p.m. If you wanted a drink after that you had to go to a nightclub.

This all changed in 2005 with a new act that saw the scrapping of restrictions and the theoretical possibility of 24-hour-drinking, although most pubs sensibly decided against that move.

Some politicians and campaigners were outraged, citing the prospect of increased binge drinking and the likelihood of greater violence on the streets due to large numbers of people getting pie-eyed and scrapping outdoors. Others argued that this was less likely than under the old system, when lots of argumentative and aggressive drunks were forced out onto the streets at exactly the same time.

As it turned out, most pubs carried on closing at their usual hour, while a few others served further into the night, causing the demise of many an old sticky-carpeted nightclub. The forecasted riotous increase in violence didn't materialise either.

LEGAL DRINKING AGE AROUND THE WORLD

The inhabitants of many countries enjoy drinking beer, but they seem to have wildly varying views on when their citizens should be classed as old enough to have one. The prize for starting them young goes to Ethiopia, where 15-year-olds are allowed to start quaffing the stuff.

In the USA, things were always much tighter: you have to be 21 over there in order to drink a beer. This might have something to do with the size of the place and the fact that your 'local' could be several miles away, so you probably have to drive there. Sensibly, US authorities do not want to see drunk and irresponsible young people in charge of a deadly weapon like a car or truck until they are old enough to make informed, sober and responsible decisions.

Funnily enough, it *is* permitted to own a gun once you are 18, putting a kid in the strange position of being able to legally fire a deadly weapon three years before they've had their first sip of beer.

Of course, that's only federal law. State law varies. In New York and Alaska you can sell a rifle to someone over the age of 16, while in Minnesota, Maine and Vermont, you can sell a rifle to someone over the age of 14 without the need for parental consent. Strangely, it is sometimes easier for a youngster to buy a rifle or even an assault rifle, rather than a handgun. I suppose we should be grateful that those teenaged gun owners aren't all completely pissed as well.

The USA isn't the only country with a killjoy attitude that prevents you from having a legal beer until you're 21. In parts of India you have to be 25.*

Legal Drinking Age Around the World

15	16	17	18	19 (WEIRDLY)	20	21	25
ETHIOPIA	ITALY	BRUNEI	UK	CANADA	JAPAN	USA	INDIA
	SPAIN	GAMBIA	AUSTRALIA	SOUTH KOREA	THAILAND	INDONESIA	
	SWITZERLAND	MALTA	RUSSIA			SRI LANKA	
	BELGIUM		ARGENTINA				
	SERBIA		CHINA				
	LUXEMBOURG		HONG KONG				
	ZIMBABWE		MALAYSIA				
	CUBA		NEPAL				
			SOUTH AFRICA				

* Depending on the state, the age in India can be anything from 18 up to 25.

CRUEL AND UNUSUAL:
THE PUNISHMENTS
FOR DRUNKENNESS

And no, I am not talking about a hangover, which some would say is punishment enough. There are more official punishments for being drunk, in this country and others.

In the UK you can be charged with being either 'drunk and disorderly' or 'drunk and incapable in a public place'. The latter means losing control of your physical or mental functions – limbs, brain etc. – and they will probably find you lying in the street or fast asleep in a skip. The former covers a range of offences, but basically means you are being a bloody nuisance and they have to lock you up to avoid you becoming a danger to yourself or anyone else. Usually this will result in an appearance before a magistrate, a stern lecture and probably only a fine, unless you do it every week.

In the Middle Ages you might not have been so lucky and would likely have been pilloried or publicly humiliated. Appropriately, the authorities used something called a 'drunkard's cloak' to carry out this punishment, which was basically a beer barrel that was altered, so that the prisoner could actually wear it. A hole was cut into the top, so their head could protrude from it, and their arms would come out of the sides, while their legs would stick out of the bottom. Then this walking beer barrel would be ordered to promenade around the town, where they would be ridiculed, to their lasting shame. Makes community service look pretty tame by comparison.

NEVER DRINKING AGAIN:
THE HANGOVER

No true Professor of Pintfulness will ever experience a hangover. They may feel a tiny bit frail after a longer than normal drinking session but long-standing Pintfulness practitioners know their limits and, like finely tuned Olympic performers, are always in training.

Hangovers are nature's way of telling you that you have not yet mastered Pintfulness; in fact, you have a long way to go.

How to describe a really horrific hangover to someone who has never experienced one? Let's start with the headache, which will feel, upon waking, like you have had the top of your skull sawn through. Your brain has then been removed from the exposed cavity and kicked around by sadistic footballers before being put carefully back in and sewn up again.

If you wake with this kind of headache, the only thing that might temporarily distract you from it is the overwhelming nausea you are feeling. This will make you crawl on your hands and knees to the bathroom in a desperate attempt to head off the projectile vomiting that is about to cramp your stomach and pebbledash your toilet (if you're lucky).

I once drank with a friend who was less fortunate. In the morning he asked me and his other guest, 'Who puked up all over my bathroom?'

Honestly, convincingly and in perfect stereo we replied, 'You did.'

'Oh,' he said philosophically. 'Well at least I don't have to bray* someone.'

There is another strange and awful side effect that can come with a truly horrendous hangover: a deep-seated and desperate gloom, along with a pronounced sense of self-loathing, which can occur whether or not you have done something awful. Frankly, if you are that hungover you won't be able to remember it anyway and will spend the rest of the day trying to relive the entire drinking session, vainly attempting to recall exactly what you said and did to everyone, including your other half, friends, boss, neighbour and the person you've always secretly fancied. What lies, half-truths, evasions, exaggerations and insults did you utter while under the influence of that last pint? Oh God, you'll say, it doesn't bear thinking about.

But you will think about it, endlessly, all day.

The good news is that, in all likelihood, things are not as bad as they seem because:

a) Even when drunk, we are usually still in self-preservation mode and therefore unlikely to tell our boss to go fuck himself, or to inform our girlfriend that we really like that other girl more than her. If you don't believe me about self-preservation mode, then how did we get home when we have no recollection of it? I usually refer to this principle as 'homing-shoes', because they seem to get us back to our house unaided. Somehow, they also ensure that the items we were convinced we must have left behind in the

---

* Geordie vernacular meaning 'hit'.

pub (keys, wallet, phone, our trousers) can all usually be found on the floor at the foot of the bed, on the landing or in the hallway. If they are not there, then try looking inside the fridge, because you may well have placed them there while drunkenly trying to find something to eat at one o'clock in the morning.

b) Everyone else was drunk too and is currently experiencing the same sense of alcoholic ennui as you are.

c) No one ever notices or listens to you anyway.

Feel better now? Good.

STARING INTO THE ABYSS:
THE SCIENCE OF HANGOVERS

Anyone who has had a drink has probably had a few too many at some point. The following morning, most people will have experienced one or more of the following soul-crushing symptoms:

- Splitting headaches
- Nausea and/or actual vomiting
- Fatigue
- Dehydration
- Dizziness
- The shakes
- Post-drinking anxiety, dread and self-loathing

When you think about all of that, it does make you wonder: why do we do it?

So, what is the cause of all this human misery? What *exactly* is the science behind hangovers?

Alcohol gets into your bloodstream and, to no surprise from anyone who has ever been drunk, it eventually hits your brain. Your liver doesn't understand that you are doing this to your body deliberately and desperately tries to get rid of the alcohol before it entirely messes you up. It thinks the alcohol is a poison, so it does the only thing it can do, which is break it up into a variety of less harmful chemicals, before expelling it from your body.

The enzyme alcohol dehydrogenase converts it into acetaldehyde, which is then broken down further into acetic acid. Are you still paying attention at the back of the class? I know this is the boring bit, but bear with me. Then it is broken down into water, CO_2 and fatty acids, which the body can cope with.

The problem comes when you drink too much and consume it so quickly that the liver can't manage to break it all down fast enough. Your blood-alcohol level will then go up and you will become drunk.

So now that you understand all of the science behind drinking and the effects of alcohol, you will never get drunk again, will you?

Of course you will.

HAIR OF THE DOG THAT MAULED YOU:
HANGOVER CURES

Everyone has their own favourite hangover cure, and they are often so personal they can make someone feel queasy at the mention of them. Hangover cures are basically the alcoholic equivalent of Marmite; you either love them or hate them.

Take the classic and timeless Bloody Mary. There really are some people in this world who like to combat severe headaches, dehydration and nausea by mixing up a combination of tomato juice, vodka, Tabasco and Worcestershire sauce, salt, pepper and, bizarrely, a stick of celery for garnish. With the exception of the vodka, I wouldn't eat or drink any of those ingredients on their own, so combining them seems like a very bad idea indeed. This produces a savoury, vomit-inducing mush that I would never inflict on my worst enemy if they were hungover.

Ginger, ginseng or even mint thistle tea (whatever that is) have all been recommended as a natural cure for a hangover, but a Professor of Pintfulness wouldn't be seen dead sipping this kind of insipid witch's brew.

In Scotland it's all about the Irn Bru. Those fine and hardy folks north of the border swear by it – and possibly *at* it, if they are really hungover – but I have never taken to a drink that is occasionally described as having a taste like liquid bubble gum. Contrary to the old advertising campaign and its rusty appearance, it is not made from girders. Irn Bru actually contains carbonated water, sugar and a variety of flavourings, including citric acid. Its full ingredients list includes caffeine, ammonium ferric citrate and quinine, sweeteners (acesulfame K, aspartame), preservative (E211) and colours (Sunset Yellow, Ponceau 4R). Sounds lovely.

No one knows why it is so popular north of the border, yet hasn't really taken off south of it, but the Scots are convinced of its restorative power – and since they are a nation that does seem to enjoy a drink, who could doubt them?

NOT YOUR FIVE A DAY: THE ULTIMATE HANGOVER CURE

Being a long-standing Professor of Pintfulness, a hangover very rarely afflicts me these days, but there were times in my youth when I woke feeling as if the world had been tilted on its axis and no good would ever come of anything again. There came a point when this happened with enough regularity for the need to discover a tried-and-tested way to combat the problem.

The first step is to drink water – my drunken self always seems to leave a bottle of water on the bedside cabinet to combat middle-of-the-night dehydration – and then take a couple of ibuprofen.

Next, stagger to the shower and stand under it motionless, possibly while holding on to something to ensure the knees do not buckle. Experience the rejuvenating and rehydrating effects of the water while very possibly cursing your own stupidity in being unable to say no to 'one last one'.

The next stage involves getting dressed and out of the door, then somehow coordinating limbs long enough to get to an old-fashioned cafe or Greasy Spoon. What's needed here is not some avocado-on-toast nonsense but a damned good, hearty British breakfast, of the sort favoured by dock workers and builders. What we need here is stodge. This is not a word favoured by nutritionists (and I ought to know, I'm married to one), but it will suffice to describe the effects of munching your way through an all-day breakfast consisting of sausage, bacon (preferably crisp to the point where it crunches), fried eggs, beans, hash browns and heavily buttered toast. A side order of chips might not be a bad idea here either, as long as you have the stomach for it.

If you are wincing at the prospect of trying to eat all of that, along with a mug of coffee and (my own personal preference) a glass of very cold milk on the side, I get it. Like I said, hangover cures are very personal, but my own body always seemed to crave the feeding of a hangover in order to render it harmless. This is of the kill-or-cure school of thought and I admit that it is not for everyone.

It does take in most of the major food groups though:

Chips: carbs
Bread: more carbs
Bacon: mostly protein (I'm going to conveniently ignore the large amount of salt and saturated fat that comes with it. If God had wanted us not to eat bacon, he wouldn't have made it so damn tasty)
Sausage: see bacon (there are more grams of fat than protein in an average sausage but at this point my body is clearly craving fat)
Beans: protein, fibre, calcium, potassium and iron (virtually health food! And baked beans are usually haricot beans, which

are a vegetable, so they must surely count towards your five-a-day, along with the tomatoes in your ketchup and the fried tomato on your plate, right?)

Milk: protein

If you can polish all of this off, you are very clearly still alive and have earned the right to go home and veg in front of the TV for the rest of the day. Well done, you!

BEER GARDENS

For the handful of days each year when the UK is warm enough to sit outdoors, the beer garden is the place to head for.

Unfortunately, not only is the UK not geared up for al fresco drinking, but neither are the vast majority of its population. We tend to be pasty-faced, light-skinned souls who turn pink with sunburn before the first pint has even been consumed. I blame the photographs in brochures and magazines of all those happy, smiling, holidaying folk, who look so at home outdoors, for luring us in.

What the photos *don't* show are the many flying, stinging insects; the changeability of the British weather, which turns from heatwave one minute to monsoon conditions the next; and the absence of shade, because usually we never need any.

I was sitting in a beer garden just the other day and, within two sips of my pint, I looked up from my newspaper (yes, I am the last man in England who gets *The Times* delivered every morning) to find that a tiny fly had committed hara-kiri by diving into my beer and was trapped there, deeply intoxicated and slowly drowning. It wasn't doing my beer any good either. This is a common problem and I decided to avoid it happening again by coming up with a simple solution. Next time I ordered, I left the bar with a beer mat. I placed this on top of the glass after each sip, to protect my beer from suicidal, six-legged invaders. I could then read the sports pages in peace, while enjoying an insect-free pint.

One final important rule that must be followed by all would-be Professors of Pintfulness: never drink in a beer garden that contains a large plastic dinosaur to attract kids. If you are foolish enough to do this, peace shall never be yours.

SKOL! SCULLING OR SKOLLING?

Most people have heard of the expression to 'scull a drink' – meaning to down a pint in one go – but how did this phrase come about? It turns out that sculling might not be 'sculling' at all and could perhaps be a mispronunciation of the word 'skol!', a Scandinavian toast similar in sentiment to the German 'prost!' or British 'cheers!'.

There is a possible Viking influence here. Natives of Scotland apparently picked up the word from them and started using skol hundreds of years ago. Somehow, over time, this morphed into scull and changed its meaning from 'Cheers!' to 'Drink that large beer down in one go now!' Isn't history fascinating?

Incidentally, the Americans don't say sculling, instead preferring to use their own word 'chugging'. This sounds vaguely reminiscent of a word for vomiting, but we can't be held responsible for their verbal aberrations.

THE MATCHBOX GAME

I first came across this (far from trivial) pursuit at college. It's great fun but does require a steady hand, some concentration and a high level of booze-fuelled confidence if you want to avoid becoming the victim here.

For starters, you need a circle of friends, and I do mean a literal circle. You occupy a table in the pub and all sit around it. You each have a pint of beer and take turns to pick up a matchbox and throw it up in the air, high enough to clear your pint and land on the table on the other side of it. The object of the game is to try and get the matchbox to land on one of its edges. If it lands on its broader flat side, as you would expect, nothing happens and you move on to the next person.

If you *do* get it to land on its longer edge, the person next to you pays a forfeit equivalent to two fingers of beer, as measured by them with their own fingers on the side of their glass before they start to drink. They then have to consume enough beer in one go to clear the area covered by those digits.

Get the matchbox to land on its smallest edge, however, and they must consume three fingers of beer.

Things get really messy when the person throwing the matchbox is careless and underthrows it, and it doesn't clear their own pint but instead lands slap-bang in the middle of it. Their forfeit for such carelessness is to consume whatever liquid is left in the glass at that point, down in one. I have actually witnessed a close friend at college do this twice in quick succession, and let's just say he very quickly refilled his glass while we recoiled in horror and left the pub at speed.

LOOK, NO HANDS! DOWNING A PINT IN ONE WITHOUT TOUCHING IT

This party piece is worth attempting if you can manage it and have the stomach or stamina for a slightly unusual variation of the down-in-one. The object is to consume a pint of beer in one go without touching the glass with your hands or using a straw. It sounds impossible, so you can challenge fellow drinkers to a bet if you are confident in your glug-ability and they might very well take you up on it.

Step One: place the full pint of beer on the table in front of you
Step Two: interlock your fingers and place your hands behind your head with your palms against the back of your skull
Step Three: bend forward and downwards, then grip either side of the pint firmly with your elbows
Step Four: press your lips to the side of the glass, ready to drink
Step Five: slowly and carefully, raise the glass with your elbows and drink. Keep drinking while continuing to raise the glass with the elbows as you start to empty it.
Step Six: ensure a tight grip as you get towards the bottom of the glass and keep your mouth in place, unless you want to end up wearing the contents of the pint when you drop it
Step Seven: drain your glass and accept the applause, along with all of the money owed from the bet
Step Eight: stride from the bar like a giant (optional)

AND GOD SAID 'LET THERE BE BEER':
NOAH AND AN ARK FULL OF ALE

As well as two animals of every kind, one female and one male, Noah brought beer on board the ark. Not only that, but he brewed it himself (I am not sure how he found the time).

That's the theory from Thomas R. Sinclair, a crop science expert. 'Noah was a beer trader on the Euphrates River,' claimed the professor at North Carolina State University. He and his wife, the researcher Carol Janas Sinclair, co-authored *Bread, Beer and the Seeds of Change*, a book which looks at the impact of beer throughout the ages.

The couple detail how beer was safer to drink than water (a recurring theme in our historical look at the reasons for beer's popularity), along with its taste and delightful intoxicating effect. Their more original idea is that Noah was a beer-seller who traded kegs of the stuff from his boat. When it was cast adrift for forty days, they would have needed a sizeable amount of beer on board to keep the human crew alive until the flood waters eventually died down. 'The classical story never does tell you what they drank for those 40 days. They had to have that beer,' said the professor. 'The people of the time wouldn't drink water.'

Of course, to believe that Noah had beer on board his ark, as well as a huge number of animals, is to have faith in the outlandish truth of the ancient biblical story, which in turn is based on an old Sumerian tale that dates back many years. If you can believe in the ark then it isn't too much of a stretch to imagine some beer on board during a time when people didn't like the idea of drinking insanitary water.

To be fair to Noah, this was in an era before even the novel, let alone cinema or TV, had been invented. What else was there to do, after a very long day feeding and mucking out between 2,000 and 50,000 different animals (according to estimates from learned scholars who spent countless hours trying to calculate this nonsense)? If anyone has ever earned a beer, it's got to be Noah. Not only did he single-handedly manage to build a truly enormous boat, but he then spent weeks afloat, cleaning up after thousands of dangerous, wild animals.

A pair of pigs can produce 22lb of manure *a day* on their own, and there were larger animals than pigs on board. Imagine how much elephant and rhino shit poor Noah had to shovel or just how dangerous it would be to clean out the lions. That is a truly cataclysmic amount of animal waste, all of which had to be thrown over the side and into the flood water on a daily basis. No wonder the poor bastard needed a pint afterwards.

THE SPIRIT IS WILLING BUT THE FLESH IS WEAK: BREWER'S DROOP

'Brewer's droop' is an old phrase that describes the inability of a man to get an erection when drunk or because of a habitual, long-term overindulgence in alcohol. This has been known about for a long time, but the exact cause is less widely understood.

Hops are wonderful things that add flavour to beer, but they are so oestrogenic that they are used as an ingredient in the treatments taken by menopausal women to offset hot flushes. What's good for women and their hormones might not be so great for men. A man's testosterone levels can be lowered by hops, which also have a soporific effect that tends to encourage drowsiness. The combination of a lowering of testosterone and an increase in sleepiness means that having too much beer is unlikely to help you out on a hot date when you need it most.

Having said that, if you are stupid enough to get so drunk that you are nodding off on the train home, you ain't handling this dating lark all that well anyway and probably should rethink your strategy.

THE LITERATI

Some of literature's finest minds have been employed on the subject of beer drinking. The notion that highly educated, literate men might have put a large value on the practice of Pintfulness seems at odds with their scholarly image, but, through the ages, writers and beer have rarely been far apart.

EDGAR ALLAN POE

Edgar Allan Poe had a way with words. The celebrated gothic poet and author of 'The Raven', 'The Fall of the House of Usher' and 'The Pit and The Pendulum' was a prolific writer with a dark mind, as well as an appreciation of beer. His untimely, premature death has even been blamed in part on alcohol but, unfortunate ending aside, he seemed to have nothing but good words to say about the practice of drinking ale.

Lines on Ale
Fill with mingled cream and amber
I will drain that glass again.
Such hilarious visions clamber
Through the chamber of my brain –
Quaintest thoughts – queerest fancies
Come to life and fade away;
What care I how time advances?
I am drinking ale today.

LEGENDARY DRINKERS:
WRITERS WHO DRANK

I know a lot of writers. I don't know many who don't like a drink; it seems to come with the turf.

Most manage to restrict their drinking to normal levels, with the occasional binge at writing festivals being the accepted exception. There are those, however, who seem to be almost literally fuelled by alcohol. They use booze to give them confidence, to banish imposter syndrome and fit in, to become inspired, or to celebrate the highs and banish the lows of a writer's career. Without it they would be nothing.

For some, their drinking became almost as well known as their work. These literary legends include the following, who all died thanks to complications brought on by catastrophic alcoholism:

F. Scott Fitzgerald died at 44. He reportedly drank thirty-seven beers a day (which seems like a very precise number but I wasn't there to verify it) and was hospitalised no fewer than eight times in the 1930s due to the effects of alcoholism. He died in 1940, just as that decade ended.

Jack Kerouac died at 59. He was 47 when *On the Road* was published in 1957. It went on to sell 5 million copies but did not lead to a happy ending for Kerouac, who died twelve years later of cirrhosis of the liver, which was caused by years of excessive drinking.

Edgar Allan Poe died at 40. His alcoholism might partially explain his bewildering and horrifying decision to marry his 13-year-old first cousin, Virginia.

Truman Capote died at 57. He famously wrote the first true-crime novel after befriending one of the murderers involved in the Clutter family killings in Holcomb, Kansas. He was so disturbed by witnessing the eventual execution of Perry Edward Smith that he never wrote another book. He went on to drink himself to an early death from liver disease in 1984.

Tennessee Williams actually lived to the comparably ripe old age of 71. A lifelong depressive who was haunted by the horrific lobotomising of his schizophrenic sister Rose, who then became a shadow of her former self, Williams drank deeply and recklessly for much of his life. His intake of brandy helped to cause rows with virtually everyone he met, wherever he went.

Between them, these drunken authors produced a body of quite exceptional work. Maybe I should be drinking more.

UNKNOWN POETS

What a pity that some poems come from the pen of unknown poets. I'd love to credit the anonymous men or women who wrote these.

Some Guinness was spilt on the barroom floor
When the pub was shut for the night.
When out of his hole crept a wee brown mouse
And stood in the pale moonlight.

He lapped up the frothy foam from the floor
Then back on his haunches he sat.
And all night long, you could hear the mouse roar,
"Bring on the goddamn cat!"

'THE BEER-DRINKING BRITON', 1757

Another unknown writer but their words have survived more than 250 years:

Let us sing our own treasures, Old England's good cheer,
To the profits and pleasures of stout British beer;
Your wine tippling, dram sipping fellows retreat,
But your beer drinking Britons can never be beat.

The French with their vineyards and meagre pale ale,
They drink from the squeezing of half ripe fruit;

But we, who have hop-yards to mellow our ale,
Are rosy and plump and have freedom to boot.

GOING UNDERGROUND

There is a pub in England that is quite literally buried underground, still intact, and exactly as it was when its doors were last opened, almost thirty years ago. The Green Man in Loughborough closed its doors for the last time in 1993 but, instead of being demolished, it was left untouched, with the exception of its entrance, which was blocked off and taken apart.

Now, it is literally beneath the Carillon Court Shopping Centre. Quite why the developers chose to leave the pub in one piece like that, instead of just filling in the space to create new foundations or replacing the site with an underground bowling alley, isn't entirely clear. It is rumoured they intended to reopen the pub once the shopping centre was up and running, but that never happened.

In 2011, journalists from the local newspaper were invited in to see what remained and take photos of a pub that was once popular but is now something of an archaeological relic. Because it no longer has a front door, you even have to go down there using a metal ladder that is beneath a door underneath the floor tiles of the centre.

It's worth the trip to see the old bar and benches, as well as the pub's large medieval-themed murals, created by artist David Parry. There are no cobwebs down there, just lots of empty, dusty glasses and a space large enough for four shops to have been built directly above it. It's just begging for someone to open it up again, but that's unlikely due to the cost. Perhaps, years from now, it can be turned into a museum, depicting pub life in the nineties. Meanwhile it sits and waits, like a huge, underground time capsule.

INDIA PALE ALE

Most beer drinkers have sampled a pint of IPA at some point in their lives. Not all of these drinkers know that the letters stand for India Pale Ale, fewer still understand the reason why.

Years ago, British soldiers could be sent anywhere in the Empire but often ended up in India. Senior officers in the British army were not noted for caring too much about the conditions of their troops, with one notable exception: beer. They knew the one thing their men needed to avoid a mutiny was a steady supply of the stuff, but this presented a problem.

In the nineteenth century, it took months to sail from England to India and there was no refrigeration on board. Normal beer couldn't survive such a long journey without deteriorating badly and often smelt off.

To make it so far around the world, a stronger, more robust ale was needed. The one specially brewed for the task was christened India Pale Ale, after its intended destination. The new beer was made with more hops, which boosted its alcoholic content and ensured the beer arrived in a better condition than the weaker brews. The troops loved it (the higher strength probably helped).

Word of this new ale soon spread, and demand increased when it started to be enjoyed by drinkers who had never left England. IPA is still a popular selection in British pubs, though most of its drinkers remain oblivious to the reason for its creation.

FORBIDDEN FRUIT: PROHIBITION IN THE LAND OF THE FREE ... TASTE-FREE, ALCOHOL-FREE

No politician in their right mind would ever suggest banning beer in this country, but it happened in the USA and the consequences were horrendous. If you wanted to trace the exact moment the United States of America started to collectively lose the plot, it was long before they elected an orange-faced, racist, misogynistic conman to be their president. No, the rot set in far earlier than that.

The demise of the USA, along with the death of the American dream, began precisely on 17 January 1920, with the passing of the Volstead Act. This (at best naïve, at worst insane) piece of legislation, also known as the Eighteenth Amendment, outlawed the use of alcohol across the entire country; you weren't allowed to sell it, buy it or drink it. The nation's longest-ever dry spell lasted for thirteen interminable years.

They say the road to hell is paved with good intentions and, like many absolute disasters, this one was caused by well-meaning people. Religious prohibitionists took a long, hard look at the world around them and passed judgement upon it. They were appalled by the level of alcoholism, domestic violence and booze-fuelled lawlessness they witnessed and decided they had to act. Organisations such as the Women's Christian Temperance League and the Anti Saloon League whipped up grass roots support, until all their lobbying finally paid off and the Eighteenth Amendment was passed, banning booze entirely.

The economic crash of the 1930s was known as the Great Depression, but at least when the economy collapsed, people were allowed to drown their sorrows by then, assuming they could still afford to buy a beer. If you look at the Prohibition years (1920–33), which overlapped the start of the Great Depression (1929) and were soon followed by the Second World War (1942–45 for the US), it can be deduced that America was a truly shite place to live in for approximately twenty-five years.

During Prohibition you weren't allowed to produce alcohol or sell it, nor could you import or transport it. There was a blanket ban on the consumption of the stuff and it's hard to imagine now how that law could ever have been allowed to come into being.

Imagine trying to enforce Prohibition. At the time, there were 123 million people in the United States, just over a third of its current population of 327 million. I cannot visualise the scale of the task involved in trying to ensure that so many people did not take a drink, particularly in an era when there wasn't a whole lot to distract them, barring the radio, theatre and cinema. Life was bloody hard back then too, so who wouldn't want or need a drink?

The religious campaigners thought souls were being saved through abstinence and that social order had been improved by the closure of bars. But the bootleggers understood what the religious do-gooders never could: you cannot come between someone and their beer. They knew that the best way to make people really want something is to forbid it, and they amassed a fortune proving the point.

Prohibition actually created organised crime. Hardened, murderous criminals got together to fulfil the demands of a thirsty public and then used their bootlegging proceeds to begin a nationwide criminal cartel, which brought an almost military level of organisation to robbery, murder, extortion, illegal gambling, vice and (eventually) drug trafficking that has been a blight on the USA for decades.

In short, banning beer created the Mafia.

The lesson we should all learn from this debacle? Don't ever ban beer.

NEVER MIND THE QUALITY

There was an insidious and, some might argue, even more terrible, long-term side effect of the Volstead Act than organised crime.

Even more serious than the Mafia? I hear you cry. How could it be?

Yes, really. Prohibition led to the collapse of American brewing in the short term, with the loss of many experienced and able brewers almost overnight.

When the act was finally lifted, the brewing industry had to start again from scratch, and it was much easier for big money corporations to establish themselves at the expense of the little guys. As a direct result of this, quality suffered and so did the average drinker. The 'Disneyfication' of American brewing led to the creation of beers of such watery tastelessness that it would be surprising if anyone in the United States has ever achieved a true state of Pintfulness at all. No wonder there is so much stress, anxiety and over-medication amongst its population.

They need lager not MAGA, before every member of its population ends up truly bitter.

DON'T LEAVE ME THIS WAY:
PUB CLOSURES IN THE UK

With a cruel statistical symmetry that went largely unnoticed, eighteen pubs closed down every week in the UK in 2018. The closure of each one was a metaphorical stake through the heart of its community and will have caused mourning. There are few sadder sights than a pub you used to frequent closing its door for the very last time. Sometimes these buildings are renovated to become desirable family homes but keep the pub sign, which hangs on their house forever: a posthumous memorial for a ghost-pub.

This, of course, could be averted, if we could start to see pubs as community assets and not just somewhere to while away the days or waste our youth in. We are always being urged to support local businesses – and what could be more of a local business than your local? How about, for every tenner you spend on Amazon, you resolve to buy a pint in your favourite pub? What if, instead of putting those worthy posts on Facebook about not sending Christmas cards but donating to charity this year, you proclaim the fact that you are investing in something almost as important? Simply cut and paste the following:

> I won't be sending Christmas cards to friends and family this year. Instead, I will be taking the money I save to my local pub, the [INSERT PUB NAME HERE]. I will be using it to help the landlord in his quest to turn a profit, thus avoiding an inevitable closure that will leave a gaping chasm in our community.

The good news is that there are still 40,000 pubs in the UK left to choose from. Each of them has managed to survive the ruthlessly Darwinian experience of operating in a depressed market with higher business rates, lower profit margins, increased competition from other forms of entertainment and cheap supermarket drinks. Meanwhile, a younger generation operates under the delusion that Pintfulness is an art that should remain lost.

All of this is a testimony to the durability and appeal of these surviving pubs. Go out there and enjoy these hardy perennials, so we never lose them.

OH, WHAT HAPPENED TO YOU:
THE LIKELY LADS

You could not find a better illustration of the emotion involved in the death of a much-loved pub than in the film version of the long-running sixties and seventies sitcom *The Likely Lads*. There is a poignant scene in which our two working-class heroes, Bob and Terry, witness the demolition of their local boozer in Newcastle, when it is torn down as part of an urban renewal programme.

Just before the pub is finally destroyed, they go in for a final pint and to discuss its imminent demise. The landlord gives them the dartboard as a souvenir of the place where they have whiled away many a pleasant hour drinking as younger men.

Even for that time, The Fat Ox is a small, old, dingy-looking pub situated at the end of a doomed row of terraced houses. It doesn't matter though. The death of this pub signals the end of an era, the removal of something tangible and solid that has always been there for them, through thick and thin. Bob and Terry are sad about this, even as they acknowledge the limitations of the place. Many a middle-aged man has experienced a similar jolt when they learn that a much-loved watering hole has disappeared.

Dick Clement and Ian La Frenais are too good at this writing game to leave you with a scene filled with cloying sentimentality, however. By the end of it, the pub has been reduced to a pile of bricks, with Bob and Terry left standing nearby, still clutching the dartboard. Perhaps though, their sentimentality for the old place is misplaced and nostalgia stops them from truly enjoying the benefits of a new era. When Joe, the landlord, approaches them by the rubble and pleads that the boys come and visit him in his new pub, they ask him what it's like.

'A bloody sight better than this one,' he tells them firmly, without so much as a backward glance.

Like the saying goes, 'Nostalgia ain't what it used to be.'

CARE IN THE COMMUNITY:
COMMUNITY PUBS

'I'm not doing it for me you understand, I'm doing this for the community. It's history, it's our heritage. I'm preserving this pub for our children and our children's children.'

Some people volunteer to work in charity shops or for the National Trust, while others run 'community pubs' – and God bless every last one of them for their tireless and dedicated public service. If I was in charge of the Queen's Honours List, I would give an OBE to anyone who prevented a doomed pub in their village from closing its doors by taking it on themselves. Is there a more noble pursuit? I can't think of one.

WHAT COULD GO WRONG?
HOME BREW: A CAUTIONARY TALE

Beer is pretty expensive in pubs but cheap and easy to make with a basic home brew kit, so why not give that a go? What could possibly go wrong?

Lots of things, including beer that tastes like it was brewed in a sweaty sock, and exploding bottles.

I had a mate many years ago at college who decided he could no longer afford to drink beer in pubs. It was too expensive, he reasoned, and he could surely make his own, so he did. The first batch wasn't at all bad, surprisingly. But then, for some reason known only to him, he decided to greatly increase the sugar content in the second batch.

This is the one that I tasted. We might only have drunk a bottle or two each – that's my recollection, anyway, but I don't recall much at all about that evening. It's the sugar that turns into alcohol, so I am guessing his beer was about 25 per cent proof, so annihilated did we become after drinking relatively small quantities of it.

Evidence of our drunkenness was clear to see the next day, when we woke to find a large five-a-side goal (complete with net) purloined from a local sports centre, in the passage that ran between our front door and the cellar. No one knew why the three of us thought it would be a good idea to walk half a mile down the canal path, scale a 10ft-high, wire perimeter fence then climb back over it again with the goal posts, which we *somehow* managed to haul up and over said fence.

We immediately felt guilty, he chucked away the poisonous home brew, and we resolved to return the goal posts the very next night, under cover of darkness. We waited till 1.00 a.m. to enact our plan.

At approximately 12.50 a.m., there came the sound of smashing glass and a ringing burglar alarm nearby, which indicated that a bunch of even bigger morons than us had decided to choose that exact moment of that particular night to break into the convenience store across the road. We were so close we could actually witness everything from my mate's bedroom window, but the last thing we wanted to see was the police arrive – particularly if they decided to knock on the door of the house opposite looking for witnesses, then accidently discover stolen property in the passageway.

We spent an uncomfortable hour waiting for the police to arrive (they did not) and the alarm to be silenced (it was eventually) before grabbing either end of the goal and running with it back along the canal bank and leaving it close to the five-a-side court. We were too sober to risk climbing the fence again. I can only imagine the look on the groundsman's face when he saw it there in the morning.

I have never drunk home brew since.

Like drugs bought from strangers, the problem with home brew is that you just don't know what's in it. This was a hard lesson learned.

Then there are bottles that turn into bombs, the home brew equivalent of a Molotov cocktail. This is quite a common occurrence.

Why do home brew bottles regularly explode? This is caused by over-carbonisation or, to put it another way, having too much fizz in your home brew. If you get your timing wrong and bottle your beer before it is fully fermented, the fermentation process will continue after it has gone into a sealed bottle. CO_2 then builds up inside it until – 'bang!', your garage, shed or kitchen is showered with broken glass and covered in sticky pools of undrinkable beer.

All of this explains why so many people attempt home-brewing once but never again thereafter. Personally, I'm thinking, leave it up to the professionals.

LET IT SNOW: THE BIGGEST BEER BRANDS IN THE WORLD

In 2017, annual worldwide beer sales amounted to an eye-watering $660 billion. Many of these brands are household names, but you would be surprised by some of them. I'm willing to bet that most UK beer drinkers have never even heard of the best-selling beer brand in the world.

The most popular beers based on sales by millions of hectolitres are:

1. 'Snow' – admit it. You've never seen one, much less drunk one, and if you claim otherwise, you are either lying or have been to China. Snow is only available there and was originally brewed in Shenyang. The beer's colossal sales can be explained by the population of China, which is around 1.4 billion people.
2. Budweiser*
3. Tsingtao
4. Bud Light*
5. Skol
6. Heineken
7. Harbin
8. Yanjing
9. Corona
10. Coors Light

*If you were to combine the sales of Budweiser and Bud Light, they would jointly take the number one spot from the Chinese beer.

BEER WARS:
BUDWEISER VS BUDWEISER

A while back now, an unseemly scuffle broke out between two rival breweries, in different parts of the world. Both use the same name for their beer and the row has dragged on for years and years.

In America, they have been making Budweiser beer since 1876. Their argument is they have been doing it longer than their Czech rivals in Budvar and should be allowed sole use of the name Budweiser.

In response, Budvar state that their beer is brewed in Budweis, so it should reasonably be called Budweiser, regardless of the American monolith already using the word thousands of miles away. Brewing in Budweis dates all the way back to the thirteenth century, and Budvar argue that Budweiser is therefore a phrase with a specific geographical connotation, like Champagne or Cumberland Sausage.

In 1907, the brewers reached an agreement that allowed Anheuser-Busch to use the word Budweiser in North America while Budvar claimed it in Europe, and that should have been the end of the matter. Since then, however, the argument has continued to rage and there have been approximately 100 legal disputes around the world regarding the right to use the coveted Budweiser name. In the EU Budvar have managed to secure official 'Protected Geographical Location' status for their beer, but in the US, they lost the right to use the name, and have to market their beer there as 'Czechvar'.

In the UK, neither brewer won the argument, which is why this is one territory where you can buy both Budweiser Budvar and Anheuser-Busch Budweiser and make up your own mind about which is the superior beer.

Of course, when it comes to taste there is absolutely no contest. Czech Budweiser is vastly superior in flavour to its American 'cousin' (consults lawyers) but, you know, that's just my opinion and not necessarily that of the editor, publisher or anyone else in my county, town or house (please don't take my house).

BEER FEAR:
AN EMPTY BEER GLASS

We've all suffered from *cenosillicaphobia* at some point in our lives. This little-known but widely experienced phobia is described as 'the fear of an empty beer glass'.

That fear is magnified around closing time or at any point when there is an enormous queue at the bar. It's always best to avoid it by keeping an eye on the time and ordering your next beer well in advance.

BEER BELLY: BEER CALORIES AND THEIR EQUIVALENT

That middle-aged spread that afflicts most of us over a certain age is not called a beer belly for nothing. A Professor of Pintfulness needs to know the impact of their pint-quaffing and you would be surprised to know how many people have no clue how many calories there are in a pint of beer. Go on, guess.

There are around 180 calories in a pint of bitter or lager.

A man should have approximately 2,500 calories per day, women 2,000, so a six-pint night out would equate to more than 40 per cent of this, before you've even had any food.

If you want to try and visualise 180 calories, a pint of beer is the calorific equivalent of any one of the following:

- Two bags of popcorn
- Two eggs
- Four plain biscuits
- Twenty Pringles

And that is in *every* pint. So, that six-pint session is the calorific equivalent of a dozen eggs or two dozen ginger snaps.

We can all manage to burn off the occasional night out, but if you drink five or six pints a night, every night, it won't be just your liver that protests. Your stomach won't like you very much either.

THE BEST PUBS IN THE UK:
A SUBJECTIVE VIEW

I like to think that, just like George Orwell, I know a good pub when I see one. However, I am not exactly entirely qualified to write the definitive list of the best pubs in the UK, since I have not yet visited them all. Perhaps one day, in a comfortable retirement that's been largely funded by the vast royalties from this indispensable little book, I will have the opportunity to complete a lifetime's ambition of travelling the country from Land's End to John o'Groats at a leisurely pace, taking in as many of the best hostelries as I can manage along the way. Until then, I can but dream. I can also give you a random list of my own top ten favourite pubs in the UK, gleaned from a more than thirty-year drinking career.

This is an entirely selective view, however, so don't get too upset if I have missed your personal favourite, and don't bother to write to me to complain because I really can't be arsed to reply to you.

LONDON

The Coal Hole, Westminster: ideally situated on the Strand, right by the Savoy, the advantages of The Coal Hole include its ability to be easily found by even a complete stranger to London, as it is on one of the capital's most famous and accessible streets. It has a good range of decent beers and an olde worlde feel to it that I have always appreciated.

The Anchor, Southwark: a stone's throw from The Globe Theatre and right on the banks of the Thames, just over the water on its southern side, The Anchor is a quirky-looking boozer, but I rarely sit indoors, preferring to take a pint out onto its terrace, which affords you an elevated view of the boats that traverse the river. If the sun is out, or even if it just ain't raining, there are few finer places to be to watch as the river rolls by.

Waxy O'Connors, Soho: the entrance to this one is tucked halfway along Rupert Street, just off Shaftesbury Avenue. It looks like a small, unimposing, Irish-themed pub until you walk inside and pass the first tiny bar by the entrance. Just beyond this is a staircase that weaves its way downwards. You will first become distracted by the tree that is growing up said staircase (you have to see this to fully appreciate it), but then will have your breath taken away by the church-style interior decor – and the fact that it serves more Guinness than anywhere else in London.

The Lamb & Flag, Covent Garden: ideal if you like your history; this one dates back to 1772. It was nicknamed 'The Bucket of Blood' for hosting bare-knuckle boxing bouts many moons ago. Now it's a good place to meet your mates for their first post-work pint but it's pretty compact and gets very busy, so most people end up spilling outside.

NEWCASTLE

The Strawberry: the best pub in the world. No, really, I mean it. I love this place. I've drunk in it for years, held book launch events here instead of book shops and been photographed behind the bar, an honour normally only reserved for former professional footballers. This pub stands on hallowed turf (almost literally) behind the Gallowgate end of St James' Park, Newcastle United's ground. The walls are plastered with signed photos and shirts worn by footballing legends, the staff are all lovely and the beer is bloody good. If I ever get to heaven (unlikely, I grant you), this is what it will look like.

Newcastle, Crown Posada: at the other end of the Toon, on the bottom of the slope that runs down to the Quayside, this Victorian pub is a magnet for real ale drinkers and people who just appreciate its unusual decor, including stained glass windows, ancient murals and a boat-shaped ceiling. The place was originally owned by a sailor; he was married to a woman in Spain but kept a mistress in Newcastle, and she helped him to run this 230-year-old gem of a pub.

LIVERPOOL

The Philharmonic: or, to give it its full name, 'The Philharmonic Dining Rooms'. Strangely enough, this place is possibly better known for its urinals than its beer. Admittedly, that's because they are made of ornate, rose-coloured marble, rather than the horrible metal trough you still find in some old city boozers. Built around 1900, the Grade-II-listed building has a musical theme and rooms named after composers, most notably Brahms and Liszt. 'The Phil' is a wonderful place to while away your time over a pint or two.

EDINBURGH

The Halfway House: situated in the atmospherically named Fleshmarket Close, this is one of the smallest watering holes in the UK. There is just one room and the pub itself is located halfway up (hence the name) a set of steps in Edinburgh's Old Town. It's extremely handy for a quick pint if you have just missed your train (whether accidentally or on purpose) at the nearby Waverley Station.

ST ALBANS

Ye Olde Fighting Cocks: this pub has a claim to be the oldest pub in England. It's at the bottom of the hill that houses the cathedral and the ancient Roman city of St Albans. Its position right by the Verulamium Park and river Ver gives it an added appeal if you fancy a pleasant post-lunch perambulation. The building – or, at least, its foundations – has been there since AD 743 but even its licence dates back as far as 1756.

HARPENDEN

The Cross Keys: I like this pub so much I put it in a book (Captain Harry Walsh, the hero of *Ungentlemanly Warfare* drinks here regularly). I do that from time to time. This one got its deserved mention because it looks as if it has hardly changed in years, and I mean that as a compliment. Thanks to listed building status, The Cross Keys can be redecorated but never rebuilt or transformed into a bland chain pub – instead, you get a real fire and bench seats close to a tiny bar. The really poignant part of the pub's interior is the large number of pewter tankards that hang from its ceiling. They all used to belong to specific regulars who no longer drink there, having 'retired' long ago, bless them all.

I could go on but I'm not going to. This is a book on achieving Pintfulness and not a Good Pub Guide. Still, I couldn't resist naming my personal favourites. I hope you like them too.

PINTFULNESS AND DEDICATION

It is hoped that much has been learned here and taken fully on board, but remember, the Art of Pintfulness must be practised on a regular basis and never abandoned or taken for granted. If you don't follow the path, your alcoholic tolerance will diminish over time – and even worse, one day, you will round the corner to see that your treasured local pub has been closed for good, its landlord and landlady forced to open up a coffee bar or teach a Pilates class to try and earn a crust. Remember to support your local business before it's too late.

Now, if you'll excuse me, I'm off for a pint.

Certificate of Pintfulness

This is your cut-out-and-keep certificate of Pintfulness.

You have reached the end of this book.
You now know everything worth knowing about beer.

Congratulations _____
you are a Professor of Pintfulness.

Use your knowledge wisely and for the good of mankind.